CW00405722

TOWN & VILLAGE DISCOVERY TRAILS

Warwickshire

Irene Boston

Copyright © 1997, Irene Boston

All Rights Reserved. No part of this publication may be reproduced, stored in a retrieval system, or transmitted in any form or by any means – electronic, mechanical, photocopying, recording, or otherwise – without prior written permission from the publisher.

Published by Sigma Leisure – an imprint of
Sigma Press, 1 South Oak Lane, Wilmslow, Cheshire SK9 6AR, England.

British Library Cataloguing in Publication Data
A CIP record for this book is available from the British Library.

ISBN: 1 85058 586 5

Typesetting and Design by: Sigma Press, Wilmslow, Cheshire.

Cover Design: MFP Design & Print

Cover Photograph: Church and thatched cottages at Welford-on-Avon

Maps & Photographs: The author

Printed by: MFP Design & Print

Preface

This book is intended to encourage residents and visitors alike to explore the fascinating county of Warwickshire. A total of forty towns and villages have been selected for their points of interest and the ease of linking those features on a short "Trail". Nearby attractions and longer walks are recommended to whet the appetite for a full day out. An attempt has also been made to spread the selection of towns and villages evenly across the county.

The Trails are designed to take between one and two hours, although stops for refreshments or to visit any of the attractions mentioned will obviously lengthen a visit. No strenuous or difficult walking is involved. Boots shouldn't be needed, nor do you need to dress for an expedition. However, it should be remembered that in winter or after heavy rain, paths across churchyards, fields or alongside rivers and canals can be muddy. Where this is likely, it is mentioned in the text and where possible, an alternative is suggested. The approximate distance of each Trail is marked on the map along with any stiles or footbridges, and if these are awkward, due warning is given in the text. An OS Landranger map adds considerably to the enjoyment of any outing. Warwickshire is covered by four; numbers 139, 140, 150 and 151. The grid references for the towns refer to the starting point of the Trail.

To select only forty towns and villages from a county rich in interesting places is a difficult task. Many people will disagree with my final selection but in a book of this size, some places will inevitably miss out and I apologise if your favourite is among them.

It is assumed that most visitors will arrive by car and appropriate parking places for each town and village are suggested. However, most villages don't have official car parks and parking on the street or by the church is generally the only alternative. Common sense and consideration for local residents are urged and please don't block farm gates or narrow lanes. If parking by the church, please give generously to church funds and don't expect space during a service. Never use a pub car park without permission, although most landlords are amenable if you also intend to have a drink or a meal. In the towns, there is ample parking to choose from.

Where public transport still exists, details are given and for all our sakes, please use it. Freed from the struggle to find parking during busy weekends, towns such as Stratford upon Avon, Warwick, Leamington Spa and Rugby are especially convenient to reach by public transport. Contact the following for detailed information: Warwickshire County Council (Traveline telephone no. 01926 414140), National Express (0990 808080) and British Rail (01203 555211). I wish you the best of luck as they all produce timetables designed to confuse rather than inform and there are many inconsistencies. As always, it is essential to check before making any journey. It's also worth remembering that opening times for museums, castles and National Trust properties change, and checking with the venue or nearest tourist information centre will save a wasted journey.

A visit to a teashop, or lunch at a country pub is an enjoyable part of any day out and possibilities in all the villages are mentioned. Individual pubs, restaurants and cafes are not detailed for the towns; each has such an enormous choice that to list everything would have left no space for anything else. It must also be remembered that I haven't tried *every* place mentioned. However tempting it might be, in the interests of research, to go on a glorified pub crawl, neither time, my waistline, nor my wallet permitted such a luxury!

A tip which may be helpful when wandering around towns. Look up! While the ground floors of buildings are mostly occupied by modern shops, the first or second storeys often retain some degree of character and clues to past architecture. Do watch where you are going though, if only to avoid colliding with a lamppost or stepping in something unpleasant!

Thanks are due to many people at various libraries, tourist offices and local history societies and especially to villagers met on my travels. Booklets produced by the churches were a mine of information. I also wish to thank my husband, Rex, who accompanied me, carried the camera equipment, scrabbled around in churchyards and dusty church corners, spotted my typing errors, and provided an invaluable second pair of eyes while I scribbled in my notebook.

While researching this book, I have visited many familiar, well loved parts of Warwickshire and explored previously neglected corners. I hope you enjoy this voyage of discovery as much as I did.

Contents

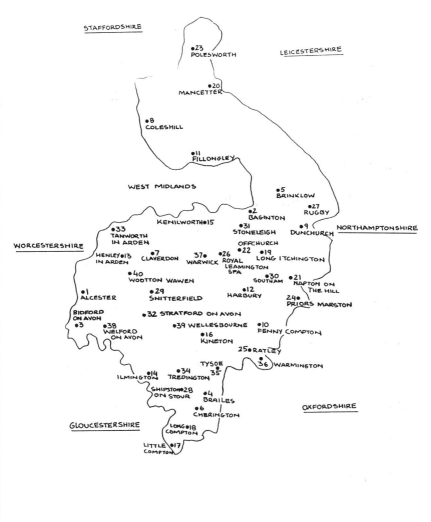

WARWICKSHIRE - LOCATION OF TRAILS

MAP SYMBOLS

BRITISH RAIL STATION	BR
BUS STOP	BS
CANAL	— — — — — — —
CAR PARK	CP
CHURCH	✝
CHAPEL	✝
FOOTBRIDGE	FB
FORT/CASTLE EARTHWORKS	
GATE	G
PARAGRAPHS IN TEXT	① ② ③ ④
POST OFFICE	PO
RAILWAY LINE	++++++++++++
RIVER	∼∼∼∼∼∼
STILE	S
TOILETS	T
WOODS	♣♣♣

Introduction

Warwickshire is a gentle, tamed landscape which rewards patient exploration. Much of the countryside is farmland (coloured green, yellow, or blue depending on which crop is attracting the biggest subsidy at the time), interspersed with hedgerows, pockets of woodland and isolated villages.

Few counties can boast such historical connections. Warwickshire's central position was of strategic importance – and opposing armies, marching from different parts of England, would eventually pass through it. Both the Wars of the Roses and the Civil War had a strong impact on the area and Warwickshire has produced many famous characters from England's past. The great Warwick the Kingmaker lived at Warwick Castle and Elizabeth I visited Warwickshire during her many progressions around the realm. Simon de Montfort, the Earl of Leicester, George Eliot, the poet Michael Drayton and of course, William Shakespeare, all have their roots in Warwickshire.

Evidence of early settlers is apparent at sites such as the Rollright Stones, Iron Age hill forts at Wappenbury and Nadbury, but other remains have been obliterated by generations of farming. The Romans left their mark through their road system with Watling Street, the Fosse Way and Icknield Street crossing the county. Castle earthworks at Brailes, Brinklow, Kineton and Henley in Arden can still be seen but it is the magnificent edifices at Warwick and Kenilworth that are justly famous. Many villages developed in clearings in the Forest of Arden, as hilltop settlements and later as estate villages serving the great houses.

Evidence of Anglo-Saxon work in Warwickshire's churches has virtually disappeared. The dominant influence is Norman which was followed by English Gothic and Perpendicular. The magnificent structures we see today were founded on the wealth generated by the wool trade.

Warwickshire has always been a predominantly rural area, the Industrial Revolution having largely passed it by. The one remaining highly visible legacy is the canal network criss-crossing the county. Along with the rest of the Midlands, canal trade has declined but pleasure boat activity is on the increase and the towpaths are widely used by walkers and cyclists.

The railways, too, have declined with many branch lines closing. Some have become nature reserves, footpaths or cycle tracks while others remain as overgrown embankments marooned in farmland. Sadly, we haven't escaped the march of bypasses and motorways and each year more of Warwickshire disappears, as man fulfils his ambition to tarmac the entire countryside.

South-west Warwickshire contains some of the county's loveliest countryside, but this sparsely populated area has a sad history. In the 15th and 16th centuries, villagers were driven out and the land converted to pasture for more profitable sheep rearing. A study of the map will reveal many sites of deserted mediaeval villages. On this western fringe of Warwickshire, significant deposits of limestone-rich lias clay have been quarried and there are still cement works in operation.

In the middle lies what is still called The Forest of Arden, even though only remnants of this ancient woodland survive. What does remain is an area of narrow, deep sided lanes, rounded hills and isolated hamlets adding up to an area full of rural charm.

The north-east is a largely man made landscape which, although fairly ordinary, is by no means characterless. Once dominated by coal mining, the deserted slag heaps still tower over the countryside, although some areas have been reclaimed to provide valuable wildlife havens and recreation areas such as Kingsbury Water Park.

In south Warwickshire there is rich farming land known for centuries as the Feldon. Dependent as much for its fortunes on the wool trade as on agriculture, in the middle ages the Feldon represented the prosperous heart of the county. The cottages are typically Cotswold in style and character and the marvellous rolling hills have been likened to a softer version of Gloucestershire, its near neighbour. The area even has its own "cathedral" at Brailes.

The lovely river Avon valley has greatly influenced the surrounding countryside. Its tributaries, the Leam, Stour and Sowe drain the southern half of Warwickshire and the Arrow and Alne flow from the north to join the Avon near Bidford. Other waterways like the Tame, Rea, Cole and Blythe head north to join the Trent in Staffordshire. Despite the intensive agriculture, there are numerous places to interest the naturalist and many of the woodland and wetland reserves are in the care of the Warwickshire Wildlife Trust. Two long distance footpaths, the Centenary Way and the Heart of England Way, cross the county and offer miles of enjoyable walking.

A relatively small area of Warwickshire boasts three of England's busiest tourist attractions: Stratford upon Avon and the castles of Warwick and Kenilworth. Leamington Spa and the National Trust properties also receive a large number of visitors. All are extremely popular destinations and less enjoyable on summer weekends when most people visit, which is, of course, the root of the problem. Elsewhere, tourists are few. Towns and villages which deserve to be better known are overlooked in the rush to the honeypots. Even the Councils and Tourist Offices promote primarily the busiest centres, and then spend thousands on studies to manage the traffic generated.

This book covers the "new" county of Warwickshire which emerged in 1974 when the West Midlands grabbed Coventry and many of its surrounding villages. Our loss is their gain and this has left the map of Warwickshire looking like a half-eaten sandwich.

Alcester

Access

Alcester (SP 092575 – OS Landranger 150) lies just off the A46 and A435, 6 miles west of Stratford upon Avon. Good bus service from Redditch and Stratford upon Avon. Also served by National Express. Large free car park (and toilets) in Moorfield Road.

The Town

Alcester is a delightful, small market town, completely unspoilt by tourism and with a rich and varied history. Even the car park has a story attached to it! The town's architecture covers every period from mediaeval to Victorian and blends together well, the only false note is struck by modern buildings. In Roman times, Alcester was known as Aluana and stood at the junction of Ryknild Street and the Salt Way. During Henry I's reign, it became a free borough and in the late 13th century was granted a weekly market and annual fair.

Lords of the manor through the centuries were the powerful Beauchamp and Greville families, both of whom had connections with Warwick. Today the manorial title is held by the Marquess of Hertford of nearby Ragley Hall (see the chapter on Bidford). Alcester has been the centre of diverse industries including the manufacture of leatherwork, gloves, needles and malting. Today, street names such as Malt Mill Lane, Bleachfield Street and Ropewalk are evocative reminders of these vanished trades.

Nearby Attractions

Two miles east is Kinwarton (SP 106584), a 14th century dovecote in the care of the National Trust. An impressive structure with walls three feet thick, it has 500 nesting holes and in the middle ages, when

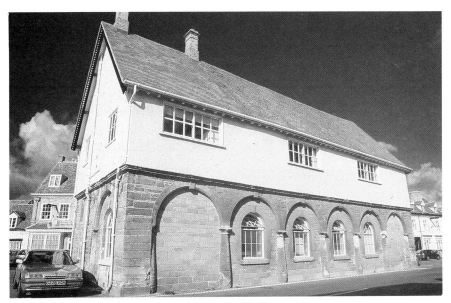

The Old Town Hall, Alcester

it was impossible to keep meat fresh through the winter, the birds were a useful supplement to a meagre diet. You can obtain the key from a nearby house.

North of Alcester is Coughton Court (SP 084605), another National Trust property well worth visiting, not least for its beautiful gardens. The house has enjoyed a remarkable continuity of tenure and for nearly 600 years has been the home of the Throckmorton family. Open from March to October, there is, as with most NT houses, a superb tea room.

The Trail

1. The Trail starts from Moorfields car park which, as promised, has an interesting history. Prior to the building of the supermarket, excavations revealed Roman remains. Amid the parked cars, it takes a huge stretch of the imagination to visualise a Roman wall and stone storehouse, today marked by strips of red tarmac. Follow signs down an alleyway to the High Street. Turn left towards the church, passing the Tudor Rose Tea Shop which is likely to lead to temptation immediately. If an excuse is needed, the fine moulded ceiling, which gives the shop its name, is well worth a look. Narrow passages off the High Street are called 'Tueries' and were once ancient rights of way. St Nicholas church was extensively renovated following a fire in 1727. The stark interior with Tuscan columns contains superbly worked effigies of Sir Fulke Greville and the Marquis of Hertford, the latter by the sculptor Sir Francis Chantrey. Tapestries, worked by local people, depict buildings and modern life in Alcester.

2. Pass left of the church gate down Butter Street, a narrow winding street which sees little sunlight making it, in the past, an ideal place to sell dairy products, hence the name. Butter Street is all that remains of a ring of houses, called Shop Row, which encircled the churchyard. Emerge opposite the old Town Hall. The lower storey, now filled in and looking rather odd, was built in 1618 and the upper storey was not added until 1641. Look inside the main.entrance to see the door to a cell which was used until the police station was built in the 1850s. The ancient tradition of the Court Leet is still practised in Alcester and each October the High and Low Bailiffs are elected, together with officials entrusted with roles such as Bread Weighers, the queasily-named Fish and Flesh Tasters and surely the most popular task, that of Ale Taster. Continue up Henley Street, passing No. 19. It was once thought that the Old Malt House, dated 1500 and seen later in the Trail, was the oldest building in Alcester, but it's been discovered that 19, Henley Street is of cruck construction and therefore older, possibly as early as 1350.

3. Cross over Henley Street and turn right, back down the opposite side, passing Meeting Lane and the Baptist Church. Turn left down Malt Mill Lane, a splendid street full of character and thankfully free from cars. The houses, renovated in 1975 and now part of a sheltered housing scheme, are very photogenic. The Old Malt House is on the right.

4. At the end, bear right, then left to cross the green. Turn right along Stratford Road to reach the end of High Street. On the left is Bleachfield Street, the part of Alcester where the linen bleaching industry was sited. At the far end is the "blacklands" which marks

the site of the original Roman development. Turn right up the High Street where, in mediaeval times, there was a Bull Ring. Continue up the High Street, where there is ample opportunity for further refreshment, to reach the alleyway back to the car park and the start.

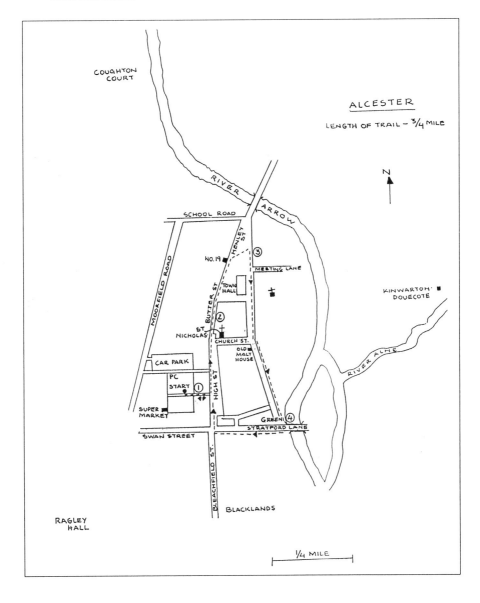

Baginton

Access

Baginton (SP 345747 – OS Landranger 140) is near Coventry airport and can be reached off the A45. If visiting the Roman Fort, a car park is available when the fort is open, (every weekend between April and end of October). Alternative street parking possible on the road towards the airport. Decent level of bus services from Coventry and Warwick.

The Village

Baginton originally grew up around the hilltop church above the river Sowe but modern development has spread down the hill towards Coventry. The remains of Iron Age dwellings, a Saxon graveyard and a Roman fort are important reminders of Baginton's lengthy and fascinating history.

The name William Bagot, who bought the manor here in 1382, will be familiar to devotees of Shakespeare as a favourite of Richard II. As with many of the Bard's history plays, the facts were altered in the name of dramatic licence, but he can be forgiven when the finished play is a work of such lyrical beauty. In reality, although one of Richard II's chief ministers, Bagot lost his castle and lands after entertaining Henry Bolingbrooke before the latter's banishment by Richard. When Bolingbrooke later reigned as Henry IV, Bagot returned to favour and his lands were restored. The castle was excavated in the 1930s but what little remains is on private land and completely overgrown. The only visible part of the castle is to be found in the church spire which was repaired with stone taken from the ruins in 1982.

St John the Baptist church

Nearby Attractions

Nearby is the Midland Air Museum at Coventry Airport (SP 355753) which houses the late Frank Whittle Jet Heritage Centre. The museum spans over 70 years of aviation development and both military and civil aircraft are on display. Open every day from April to October with limited opening during the winter.

Several miles east lies Brandon Marsh Nature Reserve (SP 385755) owned by the Warwickshire Wildlife Trust. The reclaimed gravel pits and woodland are a welcome retreat for wildlife. A token entrance fee allows exploration of a range of habitats including lakes, woodland and reed beds, and there are 5 bird hides. No dogs are allowed to minimise disturbance to wildlife. The Trust does sterling work in caring for its many reserves and protecting threatened areas against development. Membership details are available from the visitor centre.

The Trail

1. The Trail starts from the Lunt Roman Fort, which dates from AD60. Some of the timber buildings have been reconstructed and a unique cavalry training ring can be seen. Turn left along Coventry Road and where the road goes left to the airport and museum, bear right and continue past the village store and ubiquitous Chinese take-away. After several hundred yards, just past houses and before The Oak, which is a lively pub offering a good choice of food, turn right past a green. This lane leads past Oak Farm where you turn left into Church Road to reach St John the Baptist church.

2. Sadly, as with so many others, the church is locked but the key can be obtained nearby. The immense weight of the distinctive stone bell turret topped by a small spire has placed enormous stress on the comparatively small church underneath. Taking pride of place in this simple church is a remarkably preserved brass of Sir William Bagot and his wife, Margaret. Both are wearing collars bearing the badge of the House of Lancaster (Henry IV was a Lancastrian). Remnants of 14th century wall paintings have been restored and on the north arch is St Peter with his keys to the Pearly Gates. The vivid blue of the east window contrasts strikingly with the simple white washed interior. Also of note are 18th century oak panelled box pews. A comprehensive booklet on the village and church is on sale. In the churchyard are the graves of seven young Polish airmen, stationed at Baginton during World War II, who crashed nearby in 1940. Time spent sitting quietly in the churchyard may allow glimpses of birds, such as jays and yellowhammers, which frequent this fringe between the village and neighbouring farmland.

3. Use either of the two gates at the rear of the churchyard to join a footpath which borders the site of the old Baginton Hall. This was bought by the Bromley family in 1618 and later rebuilt following a fire in 1706. Yet another fire destroyed the hall in 1889, after which the owners gave up and it was never rebuilt. The site is almost completely overgrown and is, in any case, private property.

4. Bear right and then left along the gravel track which leads to a lane and past houses to the Coventry Road. Cross over and turn right to reach the Roman Fort and the start.

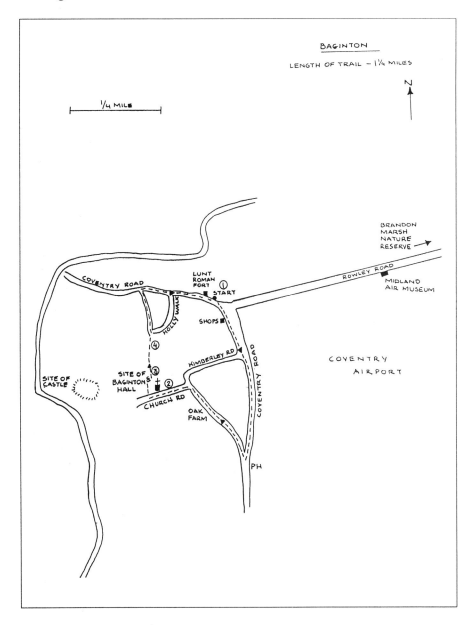

Bidford on Avon

Access

Bidford on Avon (SP 102520 – OS Landranger 150) is located just off the B439, 6 miles west of Stratford, from where a bus service runs. Parking is available in the recreation ground by the river and also by the B439 roundabout.

The Village

Bidford's history dates back to Saxon times when it was originally called Bydas Ford, developing around the point where a Roman road crossed the river Avon. In 1922 an Anglo Saxon burial ground full of artefacts, jewels and shields dating back to AD500 was uncovered. An oft repeated story is that Shakespeare and his friends became so inebriated in a drinking contest at the Falcon Inn that they slept off the worst excesses under a tree on the road to Stratford. It is believed he composed a rhyme in memory of this which ends, "Dodging Exhall, Papist Wixford, Beggarly Broom and Drunken Bidford." Today, Bidford's idyllic situation alongside the river Avon and the historic charm of its buildings attracts many visitors.

Nearby Attractions

Several miles north, Ragley Hall (SP 073555) exudes an air of grandeur and opulence. Built in 1680, the stately home of the Earl of Yarmouth houses fascinating collections of paintings, furniture and china, while the park, originally landscaped by Capability Brown, boasts a lakeside picnic area, adventure playground, maze and woodland walks. The house is open from April to October each day except Monday and Friday and the park every day in July and August. The house is also licensed to conduct weddings.

Bidford is ideally situated for walks. A pleasant path leads west alongside the river to Marlcliff. In summer, boats add to the colourful scene and keen eyes will be rewarded with glimpses of wildlife.

The war memorial and black & white half-timbered Lloyds' Bank

The Trail

1. The Trail starts by the river from the recreation ground which is unromantically but accurately called the Big Meadow. Boat trips are available during the summer. Turn left over the bridge, built in 1482, which is where the Roman road, Icknield Street, crossed the river. The bridge, with its mediaeval cutwaters, has escaped improvement and is still wide enough for single file traffic only. The pedestrian refuges, bearing in mind the speed and driving habits of motorists, are indispensable. Alas, this is not a bridge for playing pooh sticks.

2. Turn right up the High Street. There are numerous pubs to choose from including the Frog and Bulrush, the Anglo Saxon, Bull's Head and Bridge Inn and it takes an iron will (stronger than mine) to ignore the temptations of the bakery and tea shop opposite. Walk past the shops and war memorial which stands in front of a striking black and white half timbered building, now occupied, somewhat prosaically, by a bank.

3. Turn right up Church Street to St Laurence church. Although the tower is 700 years old, the rest of the building dates mostly from the 19th Century. The lychgate is dedicated to Queen Victoria's

Diamond Jubilee. Inside the simple interior is a 17th Century monument to Lady Dorothy Skipwith. The church isn't always open; at the time of writing you can gain access in the afternoons on Monday, Wednesday and Friday. You may even be able to get in on a Sunday! The churchyard stretches down to the river and is a peaceful haven with views to the Cotswolds and Bredon Hill. The bustling activity on the river provides plenty of entertainment as boats shuttle to and fro negotiating the narrow arches of the bridge.

4. Turn left up Icknield Street, passing a row of brick houses; look for the plaque above the door; Coronation Row 1902. At the junction, turn left and return along the High Street to the start. There is an alternative parallel road which does make a circuit but it runs alongside the noisy bypass, has little of merit and the buildings in the High Street are more pleasing on the eye. Besides, it provides an excuse, if one were needed, to make a second visit to that bakery!

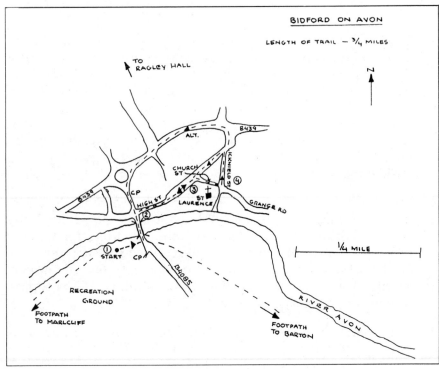

Brailes

Access

Upper and Lower Brailes (OS Landranger 151) lie on the B4035, 4 miles east of Shipston on Stour. Limited bus service from Shipston on Tuesdays and Fridays. Parking is possible in a lay-by between the two villages (at grid reference SP 315392).

The Village

Although often marked on maps as The Brailes, there are in fact three: Upper, Lower and Sutton under Brailes. Our Trail links the first two which have spread along the B4035 to become almost one village of considerable size. The villages are set in wonderfully hilly country-side on the northern spur of the Cotswolds.

In 1248, Brailes was granted a market charter and soon enjoyed a prosperous wool trade. At one time it was the third largest town in the county, after Coventry and Warwick. To put this into perspective, at the same time as Brailes was of such importance, Birmingham was still a hamlet. St George's church, of cathedral-like proportions, is fittingly known as the Cathedral of the Feldon. This place of worship is a striking reminder of the former wealth enjoyed by the community, although the extra burden of maintenance placed on the modern, smaller congregation must be considerable. In complete contrast, you can also visit a small Catholic chapel which unusually occupies the upper storey of a barn. Feldon, meaning "field-land", comprises all the fertile farmland south of the Avon and was intensively cultivated for crops until the 15th and 16th centuries when the land reverted to sheep and cattle. This is now in decline and the fields are returning to arable use.

Nearby Attractions

Brailes Hill lies enticingly close to the village. At 750 feet, it is the second highest point in Warwickshire, the highest by a few feet being Ilmington Downs. Topped by a group of trees, known locally as Brailes Clump, the hill is an excellent landmark visible from many parts of the county. Unfortunately, there is no right of way over the summit but marvellous walks on footpaths and bridleways do encircle the hill.

Winderton Church (SP 326405) of St Peter and St Paul is most unusual and enjoys a magnificent outlook across the Feldon valley. This Victorian church dates from 1879 when it was built by the exotically-named Canon E. Thoyts in memory of his parents. A notice on the door tells you where you can obtain the key.

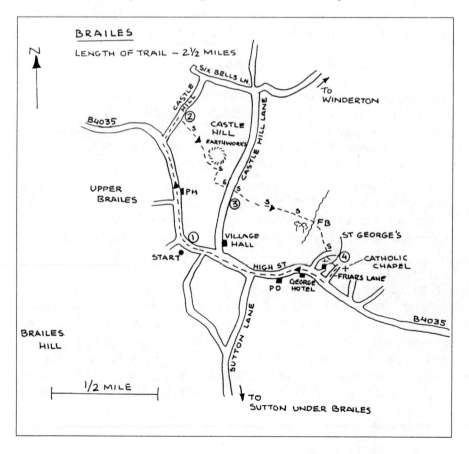

The Trail

1. This Trail, which starts from the lay-by, is longer than most and crosses fields, which means that stiles and a footbridge must be climbed. If you're unsure of your agility, stick to the main street, meeting up with the more energetic members of the party later, perhaps at the pub! However, if you enjoy country walking, you'll find this a doddle. From the lay-by, cross the road and go left through Upper Brailes. The earthworks you are heading for can be seen across fields on the right. Go past The Gate Inn and turn right up Castle Hill.

2. Almost at the end of the houses, before number 7, go down a footpath on the right and over a stile. Walk towards the dome shaped 12th century earthworks, built by the Earl of Warwick. Kids aged 3 to 70 will find it hard to resist storming the ramparts and you can take in the wonderful view across the village and surrounding countryside. The gorse bushes cloaking the hill provide a superb habitat for birds, supporting, among others, whitethroats. In such an intensively farmed landscape, any diverse habitat such as this is an invaluable haven. Pass right of the earthworks and follow the hedge on the right to cross a stile in the corner. Although the arrow points ahead, a path has developed around the right edge of the field to a stile by a gate.

3. Cross the road, climb the stile and walk straight over the field to a gate and stile in the far hedge. Follow the same line across the next field, climb another stile and keep the fence on the left, to go down steps and across a muddy section to climb a footbridge. In spring, the copse on the right plays host to a noisy rookery. After the bridge, climb the bank and aim for the church, crossing a stile in the fence ahead. St George's Church retains an air of grandeur and the massive 120 foot tower is a dominant feature of the village. Inside, the model of the church took the patient artist seven years to complete and consumed a mind-boggling quarter of a million matchsticks. Also of interest are the intricate tapestry panels. In the churchyard, amid the more conventional tombstones, is one adorned with Egyptian columns.

4. With your back to the church porch, turn left along a path to reach a small gate in the corner between houses. Walk down the alleyway to a car park with a quaint sign. The Catholic Chapel of St Peter and St Paul, built in 1726 in an old malt barn, can be visited. Walk over the bridge, pass left of the garage and then follow the signs. The chapel was of necessity built in such a secret location because of the intense religious persecution at that time. In fact, the saying of Mass continued to be prohibited until 1778 but services are still held here today. Return to the car park and turn left down Friars Lane, at the end emerging into Lower Brailes. Turn right past the memorial cross and the church lychgate, erected in 1910 in memory of a previous incumbent. Continue along the main street past the George Hotel where there is a good choice of food. Walk past the shops, the post office and along the main road lined by beautifully tended gardens. Go past the playing fields by the village hall and the unusual castellated house on the corner of Castle Hill Lane. At the next bend, the lay-by and starting point are on the left.

War memorial, Lower Brailes

Brinklow

Access

Brinklow (SP435795 – OS Landranger 140) is 5 miles east of Coventry, at the junction of the B4029 and B4027. Parking is possible on Broad Street. Buses from Coventry, Warwick and Kenilworth pass through the village.

The Village

A bustling village full of character, Brinklow stands on the Roman Fosse Way and boasts an interesting mix of architecture. In the 14th century, it was granted a weekly market and fair and, later, the development of the Oxford Canal and the railway contributed greatly

Cottages, Brinklow

to its prosperity. At one time, the Oxford Canal wound through the village bringing industries such as candle making and boat building and by 1646, the village had seven alehouses catering for this canal trade. Following the decline of such waterways, this section was subsequently straightened and today's canal bypasses the village to the east.

The most comprehensive view of the area, which we visit on the Trail, can be savoured from the top of the motte and bailey earthworks, said to be one of the best surviving examples of its kind in the country. There are ample opportunities to refill the inner man or woman with four pubs plus a couple of take-aways to choose from.

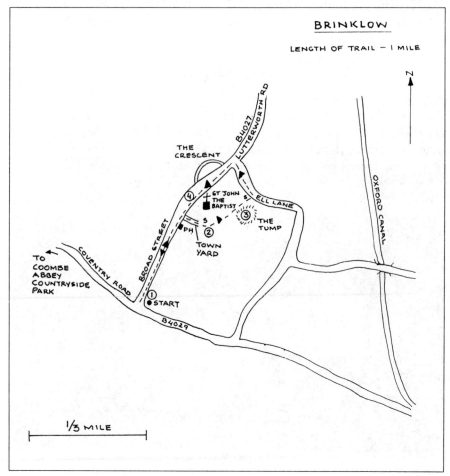

Nearby Attractions

The Oxford Canal offers enjoyable, easy walking and a stroll along the towpath in either direction is recommended.

Coombe Abbey Countryside Park (SP 405 795), to the west, provides a marvellous escape for thousands of visitors from the industrial fringe of Coventry but at weekends it inevitably suffers from its own popularity. As early as February, from a hide it is possible to obtain excellent views of the heronry on an island in the lake. Birdwatchers will also appreciate the mix of woodland and there is a visitor's centre and cafe. The old house, once a Cistercian abbey, has been extensively renovated and is now an expensive "theme" hotel.

The Trail

1. The Trail, which starts from the southern end of Broad Street, has a couple of stiles and a muddy section to negotiate but nothing too difficult. Before you start, notice the unusual village sign, more reminiscent of Norfolk than Warwickshire, at the junction with the B4029. Walk north up Broad Street where thatched and black and white half timbered buildings are incongruously squeezed in amid the more modern red brick. Of note is the Georgian Dunsmore House looming over the adjoining thatched cottages. Just past The Raven pub and before the Victorian Ironmongers, turn right into Town Yard. Walk up the alleyway and over the stile to reach a crossroads of paths.

2. Cross what can sometimes be a muddy section and go up the steps ahead into a field. Follow the clear path aiming for the mound ahead, where a steep climb to the top is rewarded with splendid views. These earthworks, known locally as "The Tump", are all that remain of a castle probably built by the Earl of Leicester in the 1140s.

3. From the top you'll be able to see the next objective, a stile in the corner of the field. Anyone who chickened out of climbing the earthworks will need to pass left of the mound to reach the same spot. Cross the stile onto Ell Lane. (From here, turning right and taking the first left will lead to the Oxford Canal). Turn left down

the lane to reach a T-junction with Lutterworth Road and turn left. On the opposite side of the road is a green bordering a row of regency properties, The Crescent. Soon you come to the church. Before you enter, take a look at No. 21 across the road where the roof is alarmingly concave.

4. The 13th century St John the Baptist Church is very welcoming and draws admiration from many visitors. Built by the monks of Kenilworth, subsequent restorations in the 15th century have seen alterations to the nave, south aisle and tower. There is a considerable slope to the floor resulting in a difference in height of 12 feet from the west to the east end. On the south wall is a little bit of Australia; the piece of black marble is from a church of the same name in Canberra. Fragments of old glass in the windows depict birds and a window illustrates the Last Judgement. In the churchyard under the horse chestnut tree in the south-eastern corner are two intriguing gravestones to local craftsmen: Thomas Bolton, a deaf and dumb woodcarver and John Blakemore, a maltster and brickmaker. Look for the tools of their trade carved on the headstones. Continue down Broad Street to return to the start.

Cherington

Access

Cherington (SP 292366 – OS Landranger 151) nestles in south Warwickshire in a tangle of minor roads off the A3400, 6 miles south-east of Shipston on Stour. Limited bus services from Banbury, Moreton in Marsh and Shipston. Space outside the church is limited but parking is possible on the grass verge in Church Road.

The Village

Secluded Cherington lies in the valley of the river Stour and the name means a village by a church. The beautiful cottages, which bear many Cotswold characteristics, are mixed with modern brick terraces and there is a popular, attractive pub.

The Cherington Arms

Cherington has almost spread to join the neighbouring village of
Stourton and it's difficult to judge where one ends and the other
begins. St John the Baptist's Church stands impressively on a hill with
glorious views from the churchyard.

Nearby Attractions

A superb walk heads south across rolling countryside to Whichford
Wood, a beautiful ancient woodland which has been managed sen-
sitively for centuries. A walk on a spring morning will be rewarded
with sightings of many birds, flowers and insects. St Michael's

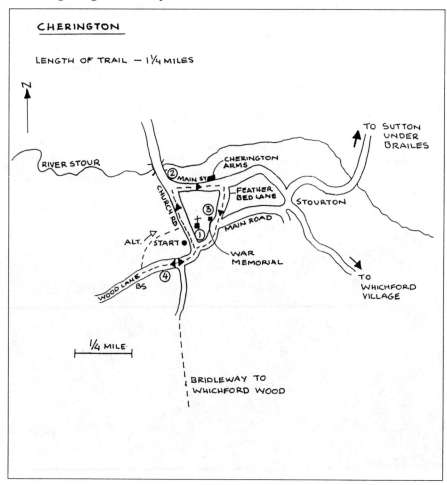

Church in Whichford is also worth a visit. In the chancel on the tomb of John Mertun is a most unusual feature. Squat down at the left end and trace the outline of a carved open book. Below is a pair of spectacles, or pince-nez, believed to be one of the first carved representations of glasses.

The nearby village of Sutton under Brailes (SP 301373) is graced by a splendid green upon which stands the Great Elm of Sutton. Now merely a stump, this venerable tree once towered over the green from a height of 150 feet but, like so many others of its type in Warwickshire, it fell victim to the spread of Dutch Elm disease in 1967.

The Trail

1. The Trail starts from the 13th century St John the Baptist Church. The interior is of pleasing proportions and contains much of interest including a carved Jacobean altar table. Worth seeking out is the stained glass in the chancel north window which includes 16th century pieces depicting the Tudor rose and the arms of France. Local tradition has it that the graceful 14th century canopied tomb is the resting place of John de Cherington, although no one is certain. The 15th century nave roof has stone corbels carved with weird human and animal heads, best seen through binoculars. If it's sunny, budding photographers will be struck by the reflections from the stained glass windows onto the surrounding stonework. Difficult to capture on film but well worth the effort. From the gate, turn right down the lane. (An alternative path from the rear of the churchyard crosses the field below, but ends in a ridiculous obstacle course. The fence, which has to be climbed, and the barbed wire topped gate are strictly for skinny acrobats).

2. At the end of the lane, turn right and walk past Wheelwright Cottage (where the difficult path comes in on the right). Just beyond is the Cherington Arms, bedecked with colourful flowers in summer. This pub also has a restaurant which offers an excellent choice of food. Turn right up Featherbed Lane. Walk past the modern red brick houses and at the T-junction, reach the war memorial.

3. Surrounded by railings, this memorial is well cared for and decorated with flowers. As with most small villages which sent brothers and fathers to war, you'll notice many names from the same family. Some villages lost a large portion of their menfolk in these conflicts. Earlier, near the seat at the rear of the churchyard, you may have spotted one such family grave bearing names you now see carved on the war memorial. Turn right along the lane and at the next junction, the church is to the right. However, continue down the lane ahead to see some of the most delightful cottages in the village. Around the corner and past the next junction are an old water trough and fountain alongside a bus shelter.

4. Clustered around this junction are a collection of picture postcard cottages, with the obligatory roses round the door and just about every window too. On the left, the Old Forge, circa 1877, stands opposite a telephone box, circa 1980s perhaps? Retrace the route to the lane by the church. (However, if retracing steps is anathema, an alternative path can be found just past the last cottage on the right. Go through a white gate into a field and bear right across fields to reach the lane by the church. As with all field paths, this way can be muddy).

Claverdon

Access

Claverdon (SP 197644 – OS Landranger 151) can be reached from the A4189, halfway between Warwick and Henley in Arden. Parking is possible at the Church Centre in Church Lane. Buses from Leamington, Warwick and Solihull call infrequently and the BR station is a mile to the east on the A4189.

The Village

Claverdon is a spacious village with a pleasing blend of historic and modern architecture. Set in large, colourful gardens in tree lined avenues, the modern houses are attractive and the whole air of the community is one of graciousness. There's even a double width of

Cottages, Claverdon

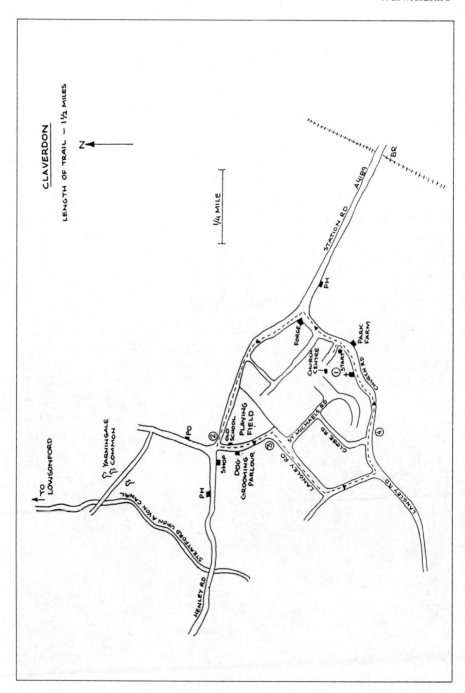

CLAVERDON

LENGTH OF TRAIL ~ 1½ MILES

N

¼ MILE

road through most of the village, all adding to the sense of space. You'll see delectable cottages with names such as Teal Cottage and Tally-ho – and Fido can even get a haircut at the Dog Grooming Parlour.

Mentioned in the Domesday book as Clavendone, a name which originally derived from "Clover Down", the village has a long history going back to the pre-Norman era. At the time of the Domesday survey, this was a small agricultural community in the Forest of Arden. Bypassed by all the ancient Roman roads, it remained relatively isolated. Even the main Henley to Warwick road is comparatively recent.

Nearby Attractions

Yarningale Common (SP 190660), a few miles north, is a marvellous area for walking where you can enjoy views across half of Warwickshire.

Stratford upon Avon Canal passes several miles west of Claverdon and the stretch between Lowsonford and Wootton Wawen is especially appealing. The split canal bridges and distinctive barrel roofed canal cottages are unique, highly photogenic features.

The Trail

1. The Trail starts from the Church Centre car park. Return to Church Lane and turn left, passing the first of many attractive cottages. Walk past tennis courts to the junction with the A4189. On the corner is the striking 17th century forge with a horseshoe shaped archway. (To the right is The Red Lion pub). Turn left along the pavement. This main road is busy but persevere, the buildings at the end are worth it.

2. At a crossroads, notice the village shop with a thatched roof, surmounted by the figure of an owl, the signature of the thatcher. We see other examples of this quaint custom in the later chapter on the Tysoes. (Down Lye Green Lane to the right is the post office and straight ahead at the crossroads is the Crown Inn, offering further opportunity for refreshment). To continue the Trail, turn left down Langley Road and pass the Italianate Old School, with

blue brick window arches. Dating from 1818, it's a most unusual style to find in Warwickshire. The dog grooming parlour is opposite.

3. Follow Langley Road past the playing field, and bear right passing the end of St Michael's Close with a good view to the church. Keep following the main road as it bends left and at a T-junction, turn left along Church Road through the older part of the village. Where the hedge thins on the right, extensive views open out across farmland. Soon you pass the end of Glebe Road. The name Glebe is very old, Latin in origin and refers to the land attached to a parish church. You'll find a great number of Glebe roads, avenues or closes scattered about the county.

4. Look for a gate on the left into the churchyard of St Michael and All Angels. The church was altered and restored in Victorian times but the earliest part of the building is the 14th century chancel. An interesting feature is the alabaster altar tomb of Thomas Spencer, the second son of Sir John Spencer of Althorp, a distant ancestor of the Princess of Wales. The considerable weight of the shield above is cracking the supporting mantle and stone of the tomb. There's also a rather snooty looking brass eagle lectern and the east window is by Kempe, a remarkable stained glass artist whose signature was a small sheaf of wheat. In the sanctuary is a memorial tablet to Charles Darwin's cousin, the distinguished scientist Sir Francis Galton, a pioneer in the study of weather and the inventor of fingerprint identification. The churchyard, with its serene atmosphere, is a delightful place to rest awhile. From the church, turn left past Glebe House and Park Farm to reach the Church Centre and the start.

Coleshill

Access

Coleshill (SK200890 – OS Landranger 139) is located east of Birmingham, off the A446. Free car parks off Church Hill and in Park Road. Good bus service from Birmingham and Sutton Coldfield and the nearest BR station is Water Orton.

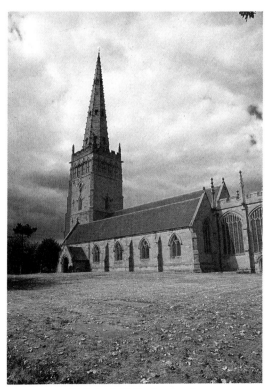

St Peter & St Paul's church

The Town

The market town of Coleshill stands on a steep hill above the river valleys Cole and Blythe, on the edge of the Birmingham conurbation and surrounded by an ever increasing network of main roads. Coleshill clings perilously to its individuality and the older part around the church has much to commend it. Signposts dotted around the town lead to various points of interest.

The Digby family were once lords of the manor and their tombs can be seen in the church. They were also notable, like Warwick the Kingmaker, for regularly changing sides in the Wars of the Roses but were finally awarded the manor in 1496 by Henry VII. Later, the proverbial black sheep of the family, Sir Everard, was executed for his part in the Gunpowder Plot. In the 17th and 18th centuries, Coleshill stood on a popular coaching route from London to Chester and at one time over twenty inns, together with blacksmiths, wheelwrights and saddlers catered for this passing trade.

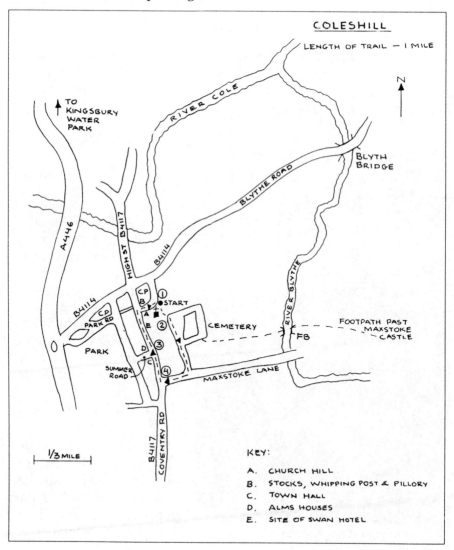

KEY:

A. CHURCH HILL
B. STOCKS, WHIPPING POST & PILLORY
C. TOWN HALL
D. ALMS HOUSES
E. SITE OF SWAN HOTEL

In Queen Anne House in the High Street the ghost of a lady allegedly haunts the stairway. Even the estate agent's doesn't escape a ghostly connection; the cottage which previously stood on the site was apparently haunted by a highwayman. Strangest of all, if you can believe it, is the apocryphal tale of an elephant which choked to death on a mangel-wurzel outside the Bell Inn on the Birmingham Road and was buried under the Sons of Rest bowling green. Try to resist the temptation to go digging to check it out!

Nearby Attractions

Kingsbury Water Park (SK 205959) lies 7 miles north of Coleshill and is a must for anyone interested in the three W's, wildlife: watersports and walking. Detailed leaflets from the Visitor Centre describe the nature trails.

A pleasant walk across fields leads past Maxstoke Castle, a fortified manor house built by William de Clinton, not the US President but a 14th century lord. Although not open to the public, it holds occasional open days in aid of local charities. A leaflet about this and other walks in the Coleshill area is available from the Borough Council.

The Trail

1. The Trail starts outside the 14th century church. St Peter and St Paul's compels attention and occupies the site of a much earlier place of worship thought to have been in existence at the time of Edward the Confessor. The interior is enriched with a fascinating collection of effigies, brasses and tablets, including cross-legged knights. (After searching for the poorly signposted toilets, I know how they felt!) Also inside is a beautiful 12th century font intricately decorated with sculptured figures. Opposite the church are attractive Georgian and Gothic houses. The Old Bank House has been preserved through the efforts of the local civic society.

2. Walk through the windy churchyard and out onto a grassed area, known as the Croft. Bear left on a tarmac path, signed Country Walk, to reach the cemetery. Turn right along the edge and

emerge onto a narrow lane. Continue ahead and at a T-junction turn right to reach the main road by the Coleshill Hotel. On the corner is a group of attractive cottages.

3. Turn right along Coventry Road, passing the toilets (yes, I found them in the end). Just past Coleshill Town Hall on the left in Sumner road is a group of startlingly unusual almshouses with mock Tudor chimneys, shields and even county escutcheons on the drainpipes.

4. Continue along the main street, passing a clutch of interesting buildings. The site of an old coaching inn, the 17th century Swan Hotel with its unusual geometric timber design, is now shared between an Indian restaurant and a jeweller's. You can still see the passageway leading through to the rear courtyard. Turn right up Church Hill passing the easily missed stocks joined to a combined whipping post and pillory, unique in Warwickshire. At the top of the hill is the church and the start.

Dunchurch

Access

Dunchurch (SP 485713 – OS Landranger 140) lies 3 miles south of Rugby on the busy crossroads of the A426 and A45. Good bus connections to Coventry, Northampton and Leamington, and it is also on a National Express coach route. Small car park in the village centre.

The Village

Dunchurch developed around the old coach road from London to Holyhead, now unromantically labelled the A45. There is mention of the original settlement, Done Cerce, in the Domesday Book and in the 17th century it was granted a market charter. The village suffered considerably during the plague which killed almost half the population. Dunchurch was also a refuge for the Gunpowder Plot conspirators in their flight from the authorities after their plan went disastrously wrong.

Dunchurch was one of the first places in Warwickshire to be supplied with gas. This was provided by a private company in 1872 even before Rugby was connected. Dunchurch makes an excellent base to explore eastern Warwickshire and retains a good selection of individual shops, with many buildings of considerable interest. In the past there were 27 pubs, which must be some kind of record. Even today, for a village of this size, there is enough choice to keep teashopaholics like me happy.

Nearby Attractions

Draycote Water (SP 466692 – OS Landranger 151), to the south, is the largest reservoir in Warwickshire and is a valuable B & B stopover for wintering and migrating birds. A small country park on the south side provides picnic areas on Hensborough Hill while permits from Severn Trent Water, obtainable on site, allow access to the rest of the reservoir.

Ryton Organic Gardens (SP 402744), west along the A45, are open every day except Christmas, and are a must for anyone interested in growing organic fruit, flowers or vegetables. There is also a shop and cafe.

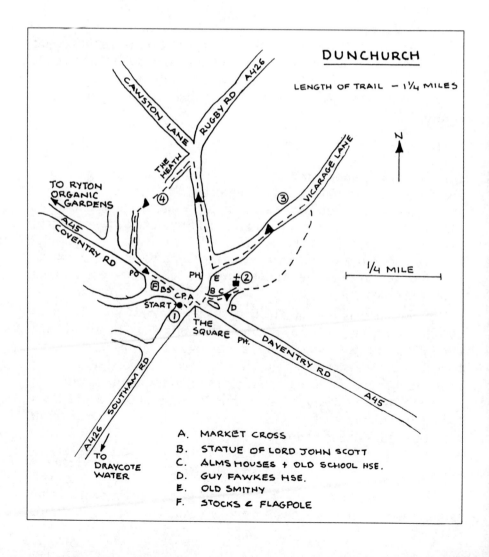

DUNCHURCH

LENGTH OF TRAIL – 1¼ MILES

TO RYTON ORGANIC GARDENS

¼ MILE

START

THE SQUARE

TO DRAYCOTE WATER

A. MARKET CROSS
B. STATUE OF LORD JOHN SCOTT
C. ALMS HOUSES + OLD SCHOOL HSE.
D. GUY FAWKES HSE.
E. OLD SMITHY
F. STOCKS & FLAGPOLE

The Trail

1. The Trail starts from the car park by the crossroads. Near the traffic lights, the market cross, erected in 1813, incorporates a milestone; although Brussels will no doubt decree these should be re-christened "kilometre stones" before long. This and the war memorial are overshadowed by the splendid statue, erected in 1862, of Lord John Scott, landowner of the local Cawston estate. Each Christmas the statue struggles to retain its dignity as it is "dressed" by local jokers. Cross the busy junction and head for the church, passing the war memorial and almshouses in the Square. These almshouses were founded in the 1690s by Thomas Newcombe, the royal printer, whose memorial is in the church. The old School House is a fine Queen Anne style brick edifice. The school building was constructed in the churchyard in 1837 but demolished in 1929, the land reverting to a burial ground. So some of the villagers are buried quite literally on the spot where they went to school, which must be quite a unique claim. On the right is Guy Fawkes House, dating from 1653 and formerly the Red Lion Inn, which, as the name implies, is the place where the Gunpowder Plot conspirators hid. Opposite is the Green Lion pub, one of the surviving coaching inns.

2. Walk into the churchyard. The elegantly proportioned St Peter's Church boasts a superb east window by Kempe depicting the Crucifixion. The church dates from the 14th century, but there has been a place of worship here for at least 1000 years, and some Norman work can still be seen in the chancel. The parish register is one of the oldest in the country. The most noteworthy feature is the tower arch which soars to over 29 feet. Three ornate bench ends are all that remain of the original choir stalls and oak benches which were richly carved. Continue through the churchyard, drinking in the marvellous views and at the rear, pass through a gate marked with a yellow arrow. Go straight ahead to a gate on the far side of the field and along an alleyway which bends left to reach Vicarage Lane.

3. Turn left to a T-junction with the Rugby road, emerging opposite a modern house of red brick with a thatched roof (which looks as ghastly as it sounds). Next door is the Dun Cow, one of the original inns which at the height of the coaching traffic could stable 40 pairs of horses. Opposite the pub is the Old Smithy, a half timbered thatched cottage full of character. It is thought that this is the smithy mentioned by Longfellow in his poem "Under the Spreading Chestnut Tree," although this particular chestnut tree is a replacement. Turn right past houses and a park, cross the road and go left down Cawston Lane and immediately sharp left down The Heath, a lane of charming thatched cottages.

4. At the end, continue ahead down a path leading past a playground and between houses. Follow the alleyway as it bends left to reach the Coventry Road. Cross over and turn left past the post office and stores to reach the green and the start. Note the Old Halt, a thatched cottage with an alarmingly twisted chimney. Another unusual feature is the thatched bus shelter, much more attractive than the usual concrete. The stocks and flagpole on the village green still survive and add to the charm of this delightful spot.

The Old Halt

Fenny Compton

Access

Fenny Compton (SP 418522 – OS Landranger 151) is sandwiched between the Burton Dassett hills, the railway and Oxford canal, and is reached off the A423. Very limited bus service to Banbury on Thursday to Saturdays; bus stop on Memorial Road, where street parking is possible.

The Village

Fenny Compton is a delightful village huddled at the foot of Mill Hill. The charming houses, of local mellow stone, line narrow lanes and in summer the immaculate gardens provide a marvellous splash of colour. Fenny Compton epitomises rural Warwickshire but is far from being a sleepy backwater. It is a lively, bustling community with a pub, school, two churches and even a fire station. Although the latter serves a large part of this sprawling corner of Warwickshire, it has been threatened with closure for some years.

The Village name which means "settlement in a marshy valley" is most apt because it has its very own water company. The supply comes from a spring in the Burton Dassett hills which is piped via reservoir tanks and a gravity fed system to a small proportion of villagers, who must be thankful they aren't at the mercy of the area water company during a drought.

Nearby Attractions

Burton Dassett Country Park (SP 397519) is an area of high, open common land offering glorious views over the surrounding plain. The hills are extremely popular at weekends and it's only in winter or during midweek that lovers of solitude can appreciate these bare, undulating tops. The pastures have never been improved and despite pressure from visitors are of great botanical interest. There is ample parking (for a small fee) and toilets. The Beacon was built in the late 14th century by Sir Edward Belknap and was part of the nationwide warning system.

All Saints' Church, Burton Dassett (SP 398515), known as the Cathedral of the Hills, was once the heart of a thriving community, which was decimated by the Black Death and the Enclosures, leaving the church isolated amid a few houses. The acoustics are remarkable and the church hosts classical concerts each year. The floor slopes uphill considerably, giving a dominance to the chancel end out of all proportion to its modest size. The beautiful white washed interior is unadorned and the lack of fixed pews gives it a spacious, airy feel. Nothing jars or seems out of place and the church is very moving in its simplicity.

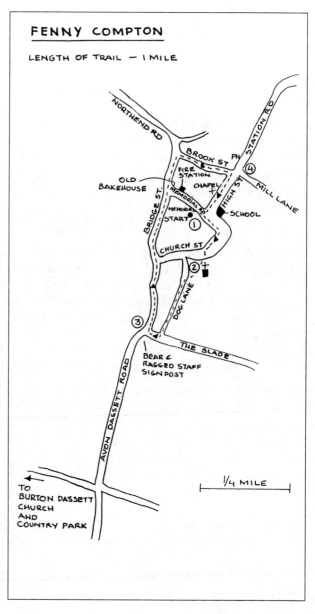

FENNY COMPTON

LENGTH OF TRAIL — 1 MILE

The Trail

1. The Trail starts in Memorial Road. With the war memorial to the right, walk up the road passing the school and bear right into Church Street. Walk past the cottages and go left on a path to the Church of St Peter and St Clare, which has an interesting history. The church is built of Middle Lias ironstone which makes it appear rather sombre and the holes on the old outer door are reputed to be bullet holes from the Civil War. The spire was struck by lightning and following repairs was left much shorter, hence the current stumpy appearance. The extended churchyard at the rear enjoys a pleasant outlook.

2. With your back to the porch, turn left along a path and through a gate into Dog Lane. Continue left past houses to a junction. Note the horse chestnut tree sheltering a seat and almost smothering a fascinating signpost; the Bear & Ragged Staff is the county emblem of Warwickshire.

3. Turn right along the Avon Dassett road, and very soon cross over to walk in greater safety on the pavement. Continue past the end of Church Street and ahead up Bridge Street, passing the end of Memorial Road with the Old Bakehouse on the corner. Proceed up Bridge Street and at the junction by new houses, turn right into Brook Street which is one way for vehicles.

4. At a T-junction by the Merrie Lion pub, turn right along the High Street passing the school and the tiny Methodist Chapel, which must be one of the smallest in the country. Continue to reach Memorial Road and the start.

The Methodist church, Fenny Compton

Fillongley

Access

Fillongley (SP 281871 – OS Landranger 140) is on the busy junction of the B4098 and B4102, 6 miles north-west of Coventry. Buses call here from Nuneaton and Coventry. Small car park next to the Happy Shopper.

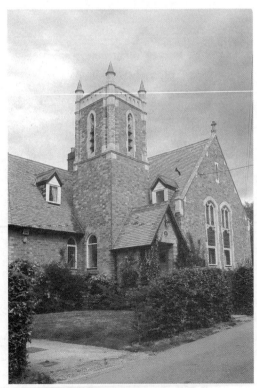

Converted Methodist chapel, Fillongley

The Village

Fillongley lies in the countryside that inspired George Eliot over a century ago. The underlying red sandstone gives the farms and buildings their distinctive colour. The village has several pubs, a Working Men's Club and it's heartening to see the post office, butcher's shop and general stores thriving. Fillongley Hall, to the west and dating from 1840, is the family seat of Lord Norton. George Eliot once stayed in Bede Cottage on the estate and it's generally believed that this provided the inspiration for her novel, Adam Bede.

In the past, Fillongley

had two castles, although only ridges and furrows betray their location on the outskirts of the village. The 12th century earthwork of Castle Hills was possibly abandoned by the time Henry III came to power; later, the Hastings family were responsible for repairing the Castle Yard site.

Nearby Attractions

Gothic Arbury Hall (SK 336892), 6 miles north-east of Fillongley, has beautiful gardens and collections of art, porcelain and old bicycles. George Eliot was born on the estate and the Hall appears as "Cheverel Manor" in "Scenes of Clerical Life." Open from Easter to the end of September, on Sunday and Monday during the afternoon.

Fillongley is very welcoming to walkers, and paths surrounding the village are well waymarked. An information board opposite the shop details possible walks in the area and the Borough Council also produces a leaflet. In a county with many footpath problems, this enterprising initiative is to be applauded and only serves to underline what the rest of Warwickshire's footpath network sorely needs. Consequently, because walking is encouraged, most paths are clearly defined underfoot and easy to follow.

The Trail

1. The Trail starts from the car park by the Happy Shopper. (The information board about walks is across the road). Turn left past the shop and cross the B4102 with care, continue down Tamworth Road past the Sunday School, founded in 1840 by Lord Leigh, whose family also had connections with Stoneleigh (featured in a later chapter). Walk past the school and the Butcher's Arms. (The pavements on this section are narrow and you may need to cross back and forth over this very busy road). Soon, you come to the 13th century Norman church of St Mary and All Saints which, most unusually, also houses the Methodist chapel under the same roof.

2. In the churchyard, amid the eye-catching 17th century table tombs is the grave of Isaac Pearson, George Eliot's uncle. One of many highlights inside is the elaborate gilded and painted stone

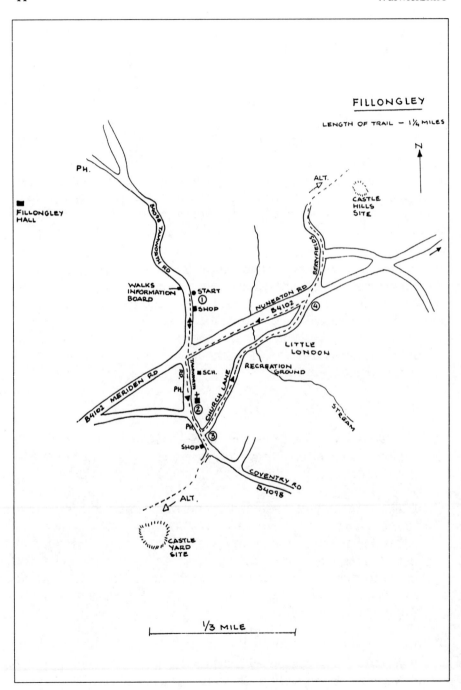

FILLONGLEY

LENGTH OF TRAIL — 1¼ MILES

N

ALT.

CASTLE HILLS SITE

PH.

FILLONGLEY HALL

B4098 TAMWORTH RD

WALKS INFORMATION BOARD

START
①
SHOP

NUNEATON RD
B4102

④

LITTLE LONDON

BERRYFIELD

B4102 MERIDEN RD

RD

MEADWAY

SCH.

RECREATION GROUND

STREAM

PH.

①

CHURCH LANE

②

PH.

SHOP

③

COVENTRY RD
B4098

ALT.

CASTLE YARD SITE

⅓ MILE

reredos, a gift of Thomas Garner, who also paid for restorations in 1887. Some mediaeval stained glass still survives in the nave windows. The church is said to be haunted by monks, and cowled figures have been seen floating around the Lady Chapel, so keep your eyes peeled. Walk past the church to the junction with Church Lane. The Manor House pub is opposite. (Just past the shop and down the lane on the right, is an inviting path, signed Country Walk, which leads to one of the castle earthworks).

3. Turn left down Church Lane, passing modern houses and the curiously named Little London cottages. This part of the village was the site of a brickworks and the pollution must have evoked memories of the London smog, hence the name. Just beyond the recreation ground is a private house, a converted Methodist chapel, which won an award for its sympathetic renovation.

4. Reach the T-junction with Nuneaton Road. Opposite is Berry-fields and a row of cottages, built in 1893 to provide homes for retired preachers. (This lane gives access to a footpath leading to the other castle earthworks). Turn left along Nuneaton Road, (B4102) past the village sign and over the bridge. Walk along this leafy lane to the main crossroads and turn right to reach the start.

Harbury

Access

Harbury (SP 373600 – OS Landranger 151) lies east of the Fosse Way (B4455), midway between Leamington Spa and Southam. Good bus service to Leamington and Rugby with a more limited service to Banbury. Free car park behind the village hall in Constance Drive.

The Village

The substantial village of Harbury is predominantly a mix of historic and modern styles, from 16th and 17th century lias stone cottages to modern brick terraces. Bounded on the east by the Roman Fosse Way, Harbury is a place of great antiquity whose history can be traced to 500 BC when it began life as an Iron Age settlement.

In the late 1920s, dinosaur skeletons over 100,000 years old were found in a local quarry and are now housed in the Natural History Museum in London. The village centre is thriving with a diverse mix of shops. The nearby railway cutting was dug in 1852 and the land either side is now an important wildlife reserve cared for by the Warwickshire Wildlife Trust.

Nearby Attractions

The tranquil village of Chesterton (SP 357582), south of Harbury, is worth a visit. The 17th century Peyto family mansion which occupied a site nearby was demolished in 1802 and the only visible remains are an archway in the churchyard and fishponds opposite. St Giles church is also of interest.

Chesterton Windmill (SP 349595) is a curious structure, not the usual windmill shape at all, which has been, rather unkindly but accurately, likened to a stone tortoise. Commissioned by Sir Edward Peyto, it may have been built by Inigo Jones in 1632. The existing machinery dates to 1860 and was restored in the late 1960s. Whatever the windmill looks like, it is a striking landmark on a site which enjoys marvellous views. Several open days during the year present an opportunity to view the internal workings.

Chesterton Windmill

The Trail

1. The Trail starts from the village car park. Return down Constance
Drive to the junction and turn right past the hall and bus stop.
Take the first left, Ivy Lane, and walk past some attractive
properties, one retains an old well outside. Reach the Dog Inn by
the Bull Ring junction and note the bull's head carving on the
wall of the house opposite. Turn right down Church Street to the
13th century All Saints Church, a wide, squat building. The
tower, supported by lias buttresses, is topped with Georgian
brickwork which sits uneasily with the surrounding stone. Continue down Church Street passing Wissett Lodge.

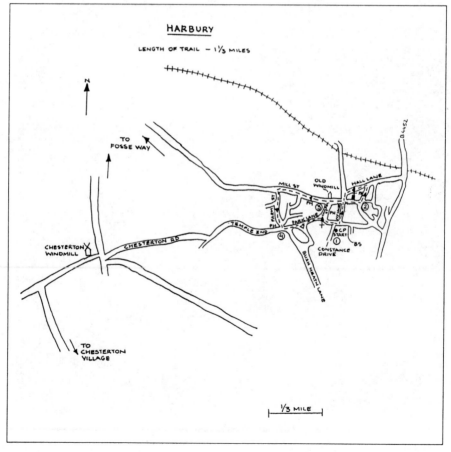

2. At the end of Church Street, turn left down Crown Street past the war memorial and an old water pump. The large mullion windowed house between the church and the Crown Inn is now a private dwelling but was once the Wagstaffe School. In use until the 1960s, it was built in 1611 by Jane Wagstaffe, whose memorial is in the church. Just past the Banbury Club, go left down Hall Lane, bearing left at the end to reach the earlier junction at the Bull Ring. Turn right into the main village centre past the old Wight School. Passing the end of Mill Lane, glance to the right at the rather unusual sail-less windmill, now a private house. The sails are said to have killed the miller and it is believed his ghost now haunts the building.

3. In Chapel Street on the left is The Gamecock pub and some interesting houses which are well worth a look. Continue up Mill Street past The Stone House and The Shakespeare pub, walking out through one of the modern corners of Harbury. Just past Yew Tree Cottage, cross over and turn left down Farm Street with its older style of houses.

4. Reach the junction by The Old New Inn (was it ever the New New Inn?). Turn left into Temple End, an area once owned by the Knights Templar order which was founded in the 12th century during the Crusades but whose wealth and power eventually led to them being forcibly disbanded. Temple End soon becomes Park Lane where you pass an impressive manor house. Go past the school and a large cemetery and chapel on the right. Bear right down South Parade which soon bends to reach Constance Drive and the car park.

Henley in Arden

Access

Henley in Arden (SP 150660 – OS Landranger 151) lies on the busy A3400, 8 miles north of Stratford upon Avon. It is on the Birmingham to Stratford railway line and bus route and makes an excellent base for a holiday. In Prince Harry Road, free parking is available, signposted from the main road.

The Town

Henley in Arden is a fascinating market town with many buildings of historical and architectural merit, all strung out along one of the most attractive High Streets in Warwickshire, which is almost a mile

High Street, Henley in Arden

long. Overshadowing the town was the castle of the powerful de Montfort family at Beaudesert, which was initially a separate settlement granted a market charter as early as 1140. Henley developed alongside the castle and became its trading centre along the line of the old main road, known as Feldon Street, out of the Forest of Arden. In 1220, Henley was granted its own charter for a weekly fair and market and since then the two settlements have been regarded as one.

Despite the rich diversity of styles, the red brick and black and white timber blend together harmoniously. Together with Alcester (in an earlier chapter), one ancient tradition still going strong is the Court Leet, which meets annually in November to elect officials. This is presided over by the current Lord of the Manor, Joseph Hardy from America, who takes a great interest in the town. Due to open in 1997 is a Heritage Centre, established by a charitable trust set up by Joseph Hardy, which will display some of the town's archives. Exhibitions will also feature Henley's recent and past history.

Nearby Attractions

Packwood House (SP 175722 – OS Landranger 139), a National Trust property, 7 miles north of Henley is open from April to the end of September from Wednesday to Sunday in the afternoons. Amid the beautiful gardens and parkland is the famous topiary Yew Garden, said to depict the Sermon on the Mount.

Baddesley Clinton (SP 202715 – OS Landranger 139), 9 miles north, is another National Trust property and an absolute gem. The house, surrounded by a moat, has changed little since the 17th century. Open from March to October, Wednesday to Sunday and Bank Holiday Mondays in the afternoons. Also worth a visit is Baddesley Clinton churchyard which is a mass of flowers in spring.

The Trail

1.   The Trail, which has a few stiles to climb, starts outside St John the Baptist Church on the corner of Beaudesert Lane. To reach this from the car park, follow signs to the High Street and turn right. If arriving by train, follow Station Road to the High Street and turn right. The late 15th century St John the Baptist has an impressive timber roof and a 16th century pulpit although the

stalls and the rest of the woodwork are modern. Walk down
Beaudesert Lane to reach St Nicholas Church at the end. Although this Norman church is renowned for its east window, the
most eye-catching feature is the magnificent Norman arch. The
church dates from the same period as the castle and was probably
built by the de Montfort family.

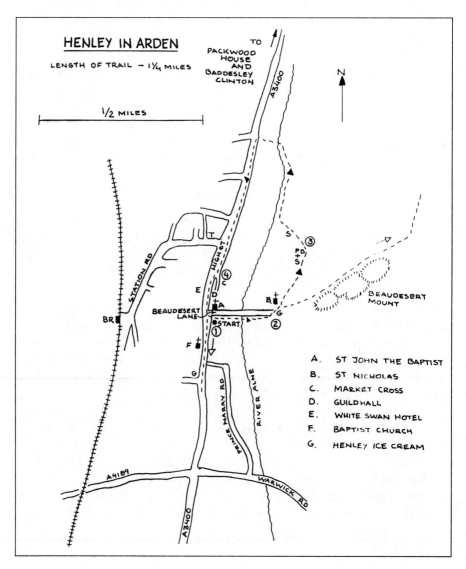

HENLEY IN ARDEN

LENGTH OF TRAIL — 1¼ MILES

TO
PACKWOOD
HOUSE
AND
BADDESLEY
CLINTON

N

½ MILES

STATION RD

HIGH ST

BR

BEAUDESERT
LANE

START

BEAUDESERT
MOUNT

PRINCE HARRY RD

RIVER ALNE

A4189

WARWICK RD

A3400

A. ST JOHN THE BAPTIST
B. ST NICHOLAS
C. MARKET CROSS
D. GUILD HALL
E. WHITE SWAN HOTEL
F. BAPTIST CHURCH
G. HENLEY ICE CREAM

2. Go through the gate at the end of the lane and left through another gate into the churchyard. The hill on the right, known locally as the "Mount" not only offers superb all round views but was the site of the 12th century castle. This was partly destroyed in reprisals after the lord of the manor, Peter, fought against Henry III and died at the Battle of Evesham in 1265 alongside his more famous cousin Simon de Montfort. Very little remains visible except the ditches which mark the line of the former moat and the rounded hilltop. A path across the Mount leads to a ridge behind Henley and offers fine walking. Follow the path ahead through the churchyard and into bushes by a marker post. The path forks but both ways lead to a field. Continue ahead, then half left on a well trodden path to reach a footbridge on the left, which in summer is often obscured by undergrowth.

3. Cross the slippery footbridge stiles and the one beyond into a field. Head half right to climb another stile and turn left, then right on a path alongside the river Alne, here little more than a stream. At the end, turn left on a concrete drive to the High Street. Turn left along the High Street, where the many pubs, cafes and restaurants offer a wide choice of food. As well as the obvious attractions of the interiors, many of these pubs have a long history and are interesting buildings in their own right.

4. Walk past the stunted 15th century market cross, surrounded by flowers in summer. Continue past the 15th century Guild Hall, which holds a collection of civil relics including furniture, pewter plate, maces and the charter that granted the town its privileges. Viewing is by prior application to the custodian at Guild Cottage, down the passage nearby. By the early 19th century, Henley was on the main coach route between Birmingham and London and The White Swan Hotel opposite was a popular venue. By 1788, a mail and four post coaches passed through Henley each day. Just past the Guildhall, you reach the church and the start by Beaudesert Lane. But it's worth continuing down the High Street, at least as far as the famous ice cream shop where many a diet has fallen by the wayside. On the way, you pass The Yew Trees, an attractive house, altered many times but retaining examples of styles from several centuries.

Ilmington

Access

Ilmington (SP 210435 – OS Landranger 151) can be reached off the A429 or the A3400, 4 miles north-west of Shipston on Stour. Buses run to Stratford and Chipping Campden. Parking is possible around the village green by the war memorial.

The Village

Ilmington is one of the loveliest villages in Warwickshire. Nestling in a fold of the hills below Ilmington Downs, this large village is typically Cotswold in character with honey coloured stone dwellings, mullion-windowed houses, thatched cottages and a beautiful manor

Postbox on the village green

house. A bubbling stream runs through the centre of the village and there are two pubs of character. Ilmington lies at the northern edge of the Cotswold escarpment and the rolling hills offer superb walking. Two hundred years ago a spring was discovered, the medicinal qualities of which were said to rival other famous spas. However, Ilmington's remoteness prevented it from developing as fast as Leamington Spa or Cheltenham.

The church, which is only accessible on foot and forms a focal point for the community, has a little bit of Yorkshire hidden away. Its splendid oak pews are the work of the "mouse man", Robert Thompson, a master craftsman in the 1930s, whose descendants carry on the trade from the village of Kilburn on the North York Moors. His unique signature is a carved mouse on all his work, and there are eleven to search for in St Mary's Church.

Nearby Attractions

Follow footpaths from the village up onto Ilmington Downs where you will be rewarded with superb views across three counties. Many circular walks are possible from Ilmington, all clearly signposted in marvellous countryside.

The beautiful gardens of Hidcote Manor and Kiftsgate Court (SP 174430) lie within easy reach. Hidcote Manor, owned by the National Trust and open from April to September each day except Tuesday and Friday, consists of a series of small gardens all on a different theme. It can be very crowded in summer and Kiftsgate with its winding paths and terraced beds is much quieter. The latter is open from April to September on Wednesday, Thursday, Saturday and Sunday afternoons as well as Bank Holidays.

The Trail

1. The Trail starts by the war memorial on the village green. The cluster of houses around the green, against the backdrop of the hills, paints a pleasing picture seemingly redolent of past centuries. Drop down across the green past the fountain, all that remains of the fledgling spa, and cross the road into an alleyway opposite. This quiet byway leads to the Norman church of St Mary's along a line of pollarded limes, twelve to represent the apostles. In your search for the Thompson mice, don't neglect the other monuments in the church, including one to Francis Canning and his wife by the 19th century sculptor, Sir Richard Westmacott, whose style favoured weeping and wailing figures. Look out for the ancient sundial on the south wall of the tower and the coat of arms of the de Montfort family, whose influence is felt throughout Warwickshire's history. The organ is modern and was built by a craftsman from nearby Mickleton.

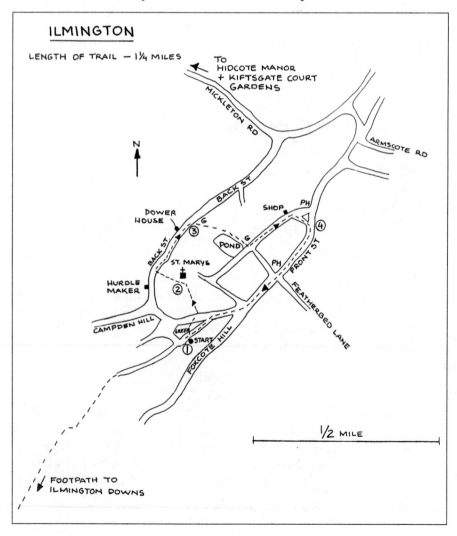

2. Continue with the church to your right, and go down the alleyway to emerge onto Back Street. A short distance along on the left is the cottage of M.D. Vincent, where the traditional art of hurdle making is still practised. Outside the workshop stands a specimen hurdle. These have been used to pen sheep for centuries and are made from both the lighter willow and sturdier ash wood. Turn right along Back Street, soon passing the Dower House, an impressive stone building.

3. Watch for a kissing gate on the right giving access to a meadow by the large village pond. Walk across the meadow keeping left of the pond, which is home to various wildfowl including moorhens and coot. Go through two gates into an alleyway with a burbling stream running alongside. This is a delightful spot, quiet and shady on a hot summer's day. Turn left along the alleyway and after two hundred yards emerge by the village shop and the Howard Arms, a very popular inn, serving a varied menu.

4. From the pub, bear right onto Front Street where you soon pass the cosy Red Lion pub. Continue past many attractive cottages, their stone weathered to various shades of gold and honey. Soon, you will reach the village green by the war memorial and the start.

Kenilworth

Access

Kenilworth (SP 285725 – OS Landranger 140) is located south of Coventry, off the A46. Free parking at Abbey Fields. Excellent bus service with connections to Coventry, Leamington, Stratford and Warwick, making this a convenient base for a holiday. Although a railway runs through Kenilworth, there is no station but there is a National Express service.

The Town

The principal attraction of Kenilworth is the castle, although the town is graced by distinctive buildings from all periods, the area around Old Town being particularly attractive. The town was once an important manufacturing centre; trades included the making of horn combs and tiles. Other industries were a brickworks, fellmongers, tanneries and a watermill as well as thriving farming and horticultural businesses. In December 1844, the railway arrived and this contributed to the town's prosperity, but the station eventually closed in 1965.

The dramatic castle ruins attract thousands of visitors each year and a whole day could easily be spent visiting this site alone. The marvellous parkland of Abbey Fields is a very popular area with grassland, a lake, trees, tennis courts and a swimming pool, as well as the ruins of an abbey and the parish church.

Nearby Attractions

Many enjoyable walks are possible with most paths clearly signposted and easy underfoot. Walk west from the castle past Chase Wood, crossing The Pleasance, the site of a summer house built by Henry V.

Crackley Wood (SP 289736), a local nature reserve, lies nearby. This beautiful fragment of ancient woodland has a gorgeous display of bluebells each spring. Woodland birds which await the patient visitor include spotted flycatchers, woodpeckers, jays, blackcaps and wrens.

Kenilworth Castle

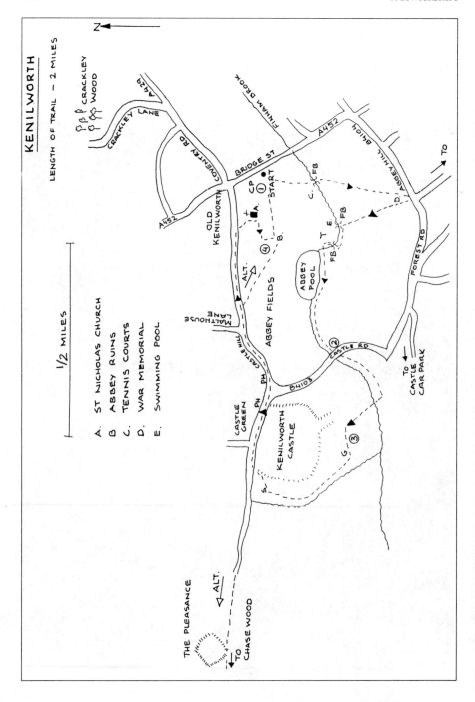

KENILWORTH

LENGTH OF TRAIL — 2 MILES

½ MILES

A. ST NICHOLAS CHURCH
B. ABBEY RUINS
C. TENNIS COURTS
D. WAR MEMORIAL
E. SWIMMING POOL

The Trail

1. The Trail starts from Abbey Fields car park. Head across the grass and over a footbridge to the left of the tennis courts. The old wall on the right is part of the abbey ruins, which we see later at closer quarters. Aim for a seat ahead to meet a tarmac path and turn right uphill to emerge by the war memorial. (The High Street with its market cross, old school house and plenty of eateries, lies ahead down Abbey End). Take the path to the right of the war memorial, heading downhill. Large areas of grass in Abbey Fields are left unmown to the great benefit of wildflowers, insects and butterflies. Turn left at the end before an iron footbridge, and take the first path on the right over a wooden footbridge to emerge by a tranquil, reed-fringed lake. This is home to a variety of birds and is a popular spot to feed the ducks. Follow the path on the left to Castle Road.

2. Turn left and just past the railings, cross this busy road with care. Head for the castle, now in the care of English Heritage, who hold many events throughout the summer, including open-air theatre, archery tournaments and displays by the Sealed Knot Society. To many, these magnificent, imposing ruins exude a greater atmosphere than more intact castles such as Warwick, and it's certainly less crowded, with space to wander. Much has been written about the castle's long and fascinating history. The original structure was begun in the 12th century and the keep was later added by Henry II. King John enlarged the castle and it was granted to the De Montforts, but when they rose up against their king, Henry III, it came under siege, surrendering six months later. Queen Elizabeth visited the castle during the stewardship of her favourite, Robert Dudley, Earl of Leicester. Her regular progress through her country must have been viewed with little enthusiasm by less wealthier lords, for a royal visit may well have cost a fortune, leaving their coffers somewhat depleted. Later the castle was "knocked about a bit" by Cromwell in the Civil War but there remains plenty to see, including the imposing keep and the Great Hall. The Leicester gatehouse and stables contain an interesting exhibition detailing a full account of the castle's history.

3. After your visit, return past the entrance railings and turn right down steps. Follow a path through a gate and around the outside of the castle walls. When the path splits, fork right and right again over a step stile and along the old moat to emerge on Castle Green, opposite the Queen & Castle pub. Cross the road, turn right and then left down Castle Hill passing the Clarendon Arms and a tea shop. Continue along Castle Hill and you'll shortly be greeted with a marvellous view over Abbey Fields. A path on the right drops steeply down and leads to the church but it's worth continuing along the road into Old Kenilworth, with its impressive collection of buildings. A path after the first shop on the right leads to St Nicholas church, and a path just by the church doorway leads right, through the churchyard to the old Abbey gatehouse.

4. The Abbey of St Mary the Virgin was founded in 1122. When the castle was besieged in 1207 by Henry III the priory was damaged by the King's soldiers. Following the Dissolution, stone from the abbey was used to repair the castle while the Norman porch now forms the west entrance to St Nicholas Church, and is indeed its best feature. During extensions to the churchyard the full size of the abbey was revealed; 160 feet long, it was one of the largest of its kind in the country. Little now remains to hint at its former glory, except a gatehouse, part of an old wall (seen earlier) and a tithe barn which houses artefacts from various excavations and is open irregularly during the summer. Return through the churchyard to visit the church. The font dates from 1664 although the base is Norman. The pulpit, screen and lectern are examples of modern 20th century carving. The car park lies beyond the church.

Kineton

Access

Kineton (SP 335511 – OS Landranger 151), 12 miles south-east of Stratford upon Avon, stands on the B4086. Street parking is possible by the church and memorial cross. Buses run to Stratford upon Avon and Leamington Spa.

War memorial, Kineton

The Village

The attractive village of Kineton lies to the east of the Fosse Way and was recorded in the Domesday Book as Kington. At one time an important market town, the market ceased trading in 1890, although the Mop Fair still visits the Market Square in early October each year. In the heart of the village, honey coloured stone houses nestle among thatched cottages and Georgian brick buildings. The village centre, with its war memorial cross, popular pubs and distinctive buildings has a timeless charm. There is much modern development in the village and a large High School caters for local children and those from surrounding villages.

Earthworks occupy a field on the outskirts of the village. Although marked on the map as King John's castle, any connection to this monarch is tenuous and it's believed to date back even earlier, possibly to Saxon times. The real site of the battle of Edge Hill was on land to the south of Kineton, now sadly occupied by the MOD and out of bounds. The baggage train of the Parliamentarians was quartered in Kineton and the village saw much bloodshed. Within months of the battle, reports of strange visions and ghostly cries were reported by the villagers, and each October on the night of the battle, the clash of both armies is said to be audible.

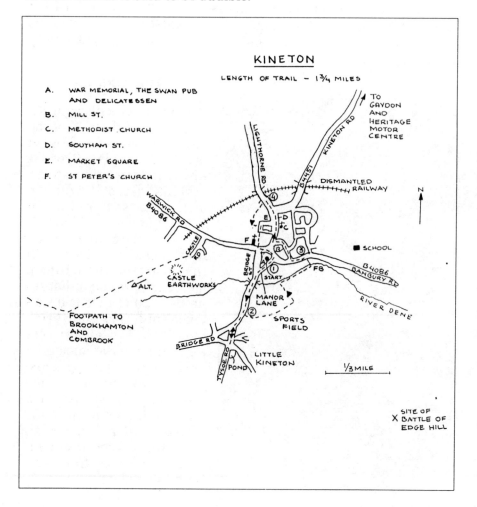

Nearby Attractions

The Heritage Motor Centre, Gaydon (SP 363547), 5 miles from Kineton, is well worth a visit, particularly for anyone with an interest in motoring history. Open all year, the collection holds more than 300 historic British cars dating from the 1890s to the present day.

A footpath leads west from Kineton past Brookhampton and across fields to the village of Combrook, with its interesting church. The nearby Compton Verney lakes are home to many birds, as well as hordes of fishermen.

The Trail

1. The Trail, which starts from the war memorial in the village centre, follows paths which can be muddy in winter but there are no stiles to negotiate. In the centre, the popular pub The Swan and a delicatessen, The Salad Bowl, cater for all tastes. With the pub to the right, walk past the cross and right down Manor Lane. At a T-junction, turn left along Bridge Road and walk out of the village, over a bridge across the River Dene, barely the size of a babbling brook. After several hundred yards, draw level with a path on the left into the recreation ground. This is where the Trail goes but it's worth continuing down Bridge Road, taking the first left, signed to Oxhill, into Little Kineton. A group of picturesque cottages cluster around a tranquil pond and village green, in the middle of which is a rare Victorian pillar box.

2. Return to the earlier path and walk onto the recreation ground. Walk to the right of the sports field to the larger building. Pass down the right hand side of the building, alongside the sports pitch. Keep the iron fence on the left to the top corner of the field, go past a sign and enter another field. Follow the left edge of the field and savour the splendid views to Edge Hill on the right and Burton Dassett Beacon ahead. Follow the path as it bends left and at the bottom of the field, turn right alongside the river. Turn left over a muddy footbridge and left up the drive onto the B4086.

3. The village fish and chip shop, the Carpenter's Arms, Londis shop and post office are to the left. Cross over and walk up Mill Street passing the village hall. Bear left in front of Battle Court Lane. Soon, bear right on a lane which emerges onto the main road by a small green and the Methodist church. Turn right up Southam Street and at a junction where the Gaydon road goes right, turn left down Lighthorne Road. The bridge ahead is over the dismantled railway which once ran from Stratford to Northamptonshire but closed many years ago.

4. Just before the bridge, turn left past a marker post onto a path between fences. Bear right in front of the wooden fence ahead and shortly go left alongside a playing field. Pass through a gate and turn left along an alleyway which emerges into the secluded Market Square. Turn right to join an alleyway which leads past the old school to St Peter's Church. The west tower is the only survivor from the early 13th century building; by 1882 the majority of the building had been rebuilt and the interior restored. The impressive 16th century churchwarden's chest, the striking effigy of a 14th century priest, carvings of winged cherubs on the front of the organ and 18th century chancel monuments are of particular interest. An excellent guide is on sale. Go past the church door and turn left to reach the memorial and the start.

Little Compton

Access

Little Compton (SP 264303 – OS Landranger 151), in south Warwickshire, lies between the A44 and A3400. Street parking is possible in the lane by the church. Buses run infrequently to Chipping Norton and Moreton in Marsh.

Memorial window in St Denys church, depicting Charles I's execution

The Village

Little Compton has the distinction of being the southernmost village in Warwickshire. It has a sleepy, unsophisticated charm and huddles in a valley below the mysterious Rollright Stones (see the Long Compton chapter). The 17th Century manor house, former home of Bishop William Juxon, has passed through many hands and is currently an Accountancy College which is one of the biggest local employers. The village still has a school, post office, village hall and bowls club.

Bishop Juxon attended Charles I at his execution in 1639 having been his close friend for many years. The Bishop lost his clerical office under Cromwell and although he was allowed to live at his manor in Little Compton, he was denied the church. However, it is believed he used to say mass in secret at nearby Chastleton House in Oxfordshire, a household with Royalist sympathies. He actually outlived Cromwell and saw the restoration of the monarchy, was made Archbishop of Canterbury and officiated at the coronation of Charles II. Sadly, he died only three years later in 1663 at the age of 81.

Nearby Attractions

The Four Shire Stone (SP 232322), on the A44, 4 miles west of Little Compton, marks the old meeting point of four counties, Gloucestershire, Warwickshire, Oxfordshire and Worcestershire, although the latter, which here accounted for only a small area, has now been gobbled up by Gloucestershire.

Over the border in Oxfordshire, the attractive market town of Chipping Norton (SP 315271 – OS Landranger 164), is well worth a visit. The Parish Church and 17th century almshouses are among the many buildings of interest.

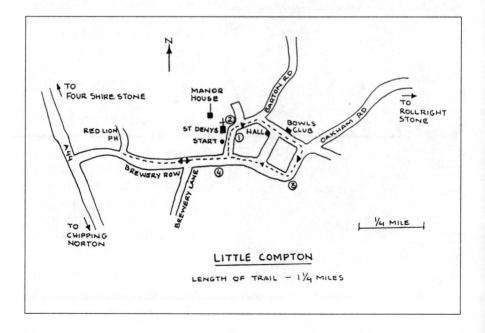

LITTLE COMPTON

LENGTH OF TRAIL — 1¼ MILES

The Trail

1. The Trail starts from outside the welcoming little church of St Denys which contains impressive monuments to the Dixon family. The 14th century saddleback tower is an unusual feature. Although the church is dwarfed by the adjoining manor house, the interior is surprisingly spacious. There has been a place of worship on this site since Norman times, but extensive restorations undertaken by the Victorians have obscured much of the original work. Of principal interest is a splendid stained glass window telling the story of Charles I's execution, showing his walk in the snow, farewells to his children, his execution and his coffin being borne into the chapel. Another poignant memorial is the glass in the sanctuary window, which was taken from a ruined church on the Somme by a local glazier whilst on active service. He placed the glass in the window as a memorial to the soldiers who lost their lives during the battle. The 13th century font is fractured and held together by iron bands. A detailed church history hangs on the nave wall. Look for the Leverton Harris tomb just opposite the churchyard seat and spot the mistake made by the stonemason. The attempted correction has only confused matters – should it be 1926 or 1927?

2. With the church to the left, walk to the end of the lane by an imposing gateway, part of the college, and turn right. A curious feature on this Trail is the lack of visible street names. Continue, ignoring the left turn to Barton on the Heath. The road bends to the right and, ignoring a right turn by the village hall, walk past an immaculately tended bowls club on the left.

3. At the T-junction, admire the delightful cottages which, in traditional fashion, are adorned with roses round the doors. Turn right and follow the road as it bends right. Pass the end of another road by tennis courts and Rivington Glebe House. Just past a playing field, reach the lane by the church and the start.

4. However, if you feel you've earned some refreshment, don't turn right but go straight on, passing another gateway to the college which allows a clearer view of this magnificent building. After about half a mile, you reach the Red Lion Inn tucked away on the right which offers an excellent choice of food. When you are replete, retrace your steps to the lane by the church.

Long Compton

Access

L ong Compton (SP 290327 – OS Landranger 151) straddles the busy A3400, 8 miles south of Shipston on Stour. Buses from Stratford, Leamington and Oxford run through the village. Parking is possible on the grass verge of Buryway Lane, just below the church, signed to Barton.

The Village

Long Compton is a beautiful village at the bottom of a steep hill and boasts a majestic church. The thatched cottages and houses built of local stone, all with lovely gardens, are strung out along the main road and the many quiet side streets are worthy of exploration. The village is rich in folklore and stories of witchcraft abound. One old saying goes that "there were enough witches in Long Compton to draw a load of hay up the hill." In 1875 an old woman was accused of being a witch and murdered by one Jems Heywood who claimed she had cast a spell on his livestock.

The Village retains a pleasant atmosphere despite the ever present drone of traffic, but spare a thought for the villagers who have to cope with the sheer volume of vehicles roaring past, only feet from their front doors.

Nearby Attractions

The Rollright Stones (SP296309), on the ridge above the village, is a remarkable Bronze Age stone circle. Known as the King's Men, it dates from around 1,500 BC but its origins and purpose remain a mystery although there's a wonderful legend attached to it. The stones are supposed to be a king and his followers. Marching along the hill they were met by a witch who told the monarch "If Long Compton thou

The King's Stone, Rollright Stones

canst see, King of England shalt thou be." A spur of land obscures the view of the village from the top, so the king and his followers were turned to stone and there they stand to this day. The main circle is difficult to photograph satisfactorily and the lonely sentinels of the King's Stone and Whispering Knights are far more striking. Choose a wild winter's day under dramatic skies for your visit and soak up the atmosphere of this eerie place.

Long Compton is set in excellent walking country; a splendid ramble leads south up the hill to Little Compton (see the previous chapter).

The Trail

1. The Trail starts on the lane where you park. Continue along Buryway Lane, heading away from the village. From this lane, you can appreciate Long Compton's situation amid marvellous rolling countryside. The ridges and bumps in the field on the right are thought to mark the site of the original village. At a junction, turn right and follow the road as it bends right along Crockwell Street to reach a T-junction with the main street, the A3400. It was hoped that the opening of the M40 would result in a considerable reduction in traffic but this road seems as busy as ever.

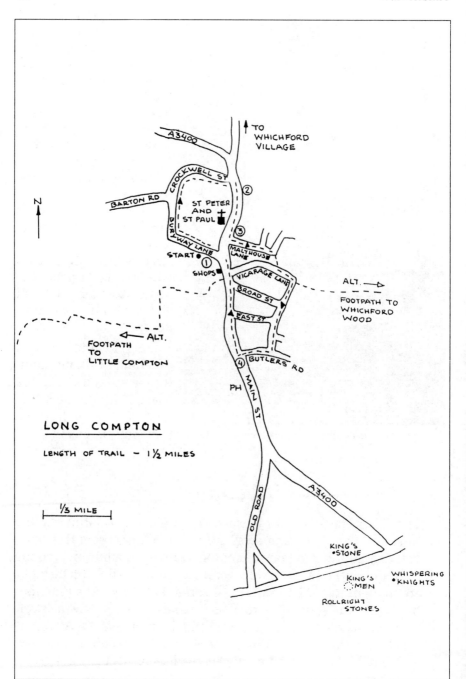

TO
WHICHFORD
VILLAGE

A3400

CROCKWELL ST

BARTON RD

N

②

ST PETER
AND
ST PAUL

DURY WAY LANE

START ①

SHOPS

MALTHOUSE
LANE

③

VICARAGE LANE

BROAD ST

EAST ST

ALT.

FOOTPATH TO
WHICHFORD
WOOD

ALT.

FOOTPATH
TO
LITTLE COMPTON

④ BUTLERS RD

PH

MAIN ST

LONG COMPTON

LENGTH OF TRAIL — 1½ MILES

⅓ MILE

OLD ROAD

A3400

KING'S
•STONE

KING'S
⁙MEN

WHISPERING
•KNIGHTS

ROLLRIGHT
STONES

2. Turn right and you will soon reach St Peter & St Paul's Church. The interior has been heavily restored in the past and the walls are bare. As with many churches, it pays to look up, this time at the stone supports for the roof trusses, with their profusion of carved heads, some quite hideous. Binoculars, or a telephoto lens, will reveal the effort put into features which would have been out of sight of earlier congregations; a remarkable testimony to the skill, and sense of humour, of the stonemasons. On the tower exterior are odd looking gargoyles with pipes protruding from their mouths, which are designed to take the water away from the surface of the tower. The most unusual feature of this church is outside. As lychgates go, this is surely a five star version, with a quaint thatched upper storey. The structure dates back 400 years and was originally a cottage, which with its lower storey removed was donated by Mrs Latham in 1964 in memory of her husband. It is an intriguing feature which catches the eye and tempts many to stop for a closer look.

3. From the lychgate, cross over, turn right and very shortly go left down Malthouse Lane. Walk down this charming lane and almost at the end, just past a house called Helens, turn right down an alleyway. This leads into Vicarage Lane; a street of idyllic old cottages and modern brick houses. Turn left and you will soon reach the outskirts of the village. (A footpath at the end of the lane leads across fields and up to Whichford Wood and is well worth following if you have the time). At the end of Vicarage Lane, turn right and follow the road. You pass Broad Street and East Street on the right, both highly attractive quiet lanes, and at the end of the lane, turn right down Butlers Road which emerges onto the main road.

4. (Here, a left turn will lead to the Red Lion Hotel). Turn right and walk back up the main road. Many of the houses alongside the road have a burbling stream running through their gardens. When you reach the shop, look for a drinking tap which also forms the base of the village cross. Just beyond is the butcher's shop, Long Compton being one of the few villages to retain its traditional family butcher's. Walk past the post office cum village stores to reach Buryway Lane and the start.

Long Itchington

Access

L ong Itchington (SP 412652 – OS Landranger 151) is on the A423,
2 miles north of Southam. Good bus service from Leamington,
Southam and Rugby. Parking is possible by the phone box near the
village green, just off the A423.

The Village

Long Itchington is a charming village standing on the banks of the
River Itchen, which gives the village its name. The village is believed
to be the 11th century birthplace of St Wulfstan, Bishop of Worcester
during the Norman conquest, who later declared his loyalty to Wil-

Village pond, Long Itchington

liam the Conqueror. Unlike many villages, Long Itchington still has shops, a post office, a school and plenty of pubs.

The Village has produced a booklet under the banner of the "Alive" Project (Annual Long Itchington Venture for the Environment). It gives details of three local walks possible from the village. This project has the worthwhile aim of encouraging visitors to explore the village and the pleasant countryside nearby, and for villagers to become involved in their local environment. Essential reading is a book written in 1968 by Archibald Payne: "Portrait of a Parish" which is an affectionate look at the history and characters of the village by a schoolmaster who spent many years there.

Nearby Attractions

Stockton (SP 436636) is an interesting village, 3 miles south-east of Long Itchington. First mentioned in records dating from 1272, it remained a tiny hamlet until the discovery of the famous Blue Lias stone. Victoria embankment in London was constructed from this same stone.

The Grand Union Canal cuts through the countryside south of Long Itchington and an attractive walk along the towpath between Bascote Locks and the locks of Stockton Flight is recommended. Stockton Flight's ten locks were altered in the late 1920s and the original old narrow locks act as overspill weirs.

The Trail

1. The Trail starts by the village pond, a delightful central feature which is home to moorhens, mallards and the resident swans, as well as two species of wagtail, pied and grey. Water lilies thrive and around the edge grow yellow iris and rosebay willowherb, while dragonflies and damselflies skim the surface. Surrounding the pond are lime, alder and copper beech trees. With the pond to the right, walk ahead across the village green and down Church Road. There is ample opportunity for refreshments in Long Itchington at the Buck & Bell, the Harvester pub, the Jolly Fisherman, plus two other pubs alongside the nearby canal. Just by the bus stop, turn right down a pathway, marked with a yellow

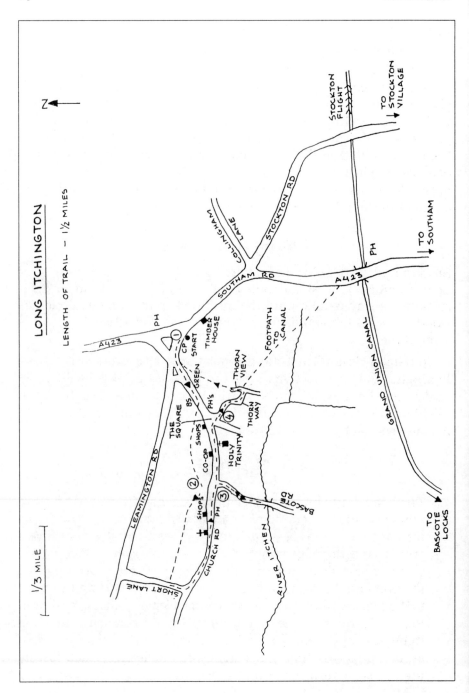

arrow. This passes behind the school, the cemetery and between some allotments.

2. Just past the allotments, turn right and immediately left down the alleyway which emerges onto a road. Turn left and at the junction, left again, signed to Bascote. Go past the Congregational Church and the Green Man, possibly the oldest pub in the village. Pass the post office, a shop and house called the Old Bakery. When you reach the end of the lane signed to Bascote, a short detour to the bridge on the right will reveal a pleasant view across the river to the church. This river begins its life to the south-east at Marston Doles before joining the river Leam further north.

3. Return to the junction and turn right along Church Road passing the Co-op to reach Holy Trinity Church. Sandstone buttresses support the tower which is surmounted by a stump, all that remains of the original soaring spire toppled during a storm in 1762. Inside is an impressive 14th century rood screen and behind the altar is a stone reredos engraved with the Ten Commandments. A stained glass roundel in the south aisle depicts the legend of St Wulfstan. Outside you can admire splendid yew trees and spend a quiet moment in the Garden of Rest. The church itself is home to a colony of bats, and when I visited, a family of swallows were nesting in the porch. Continue through the churchyard and out into The Square.

4. Turn right along Thorn Way and after it bends left, you will reach a junction of several footpaths. (The path on the right leads over fields to the canal). Turn left past Thorn View, note the arrow on the lamp post, and walk up the drive past the house and down an alleyway to emerge by the village green. Walk ahead onto the green and the start is over to the right. Just past the telephone box is a magnificent timber house, formerly the home of Lady Holbourne, which hosted visits by Elizabeth I in 1572 and 1575. Later owners included the Sitwell family.

Mancetter

Access

Mancetter (SK 321966 – OS Landranger 140) is just off the A5, east of Atherstone. The large church car park reached via a gateway *between* the pub and church is easily missed. The nearest railway station is at Atherstone. Good bus service to Nuneaton, Coventry and Atherstone where you can also connect with buses to Birmingham.

The Village

Mancetter was originally a Roman settlement, Manduessedum, on Watling Street, which is now more prosaically known as the A5. It lies in the Anker Valley, a major arterial route carrying the main railway line and the Coventry Canal to the south. Historical tales abound and it is said that this was the site of Boadicea's defeat by the Romans.

The scene around the village green is a real gem with the church and a cluster of cottages forming the ancient heart of the village. The modern corners of the community, which add little to its charm, have spread almost as far as neighbouring Atherstone, yet Mancetter still clings to its separate identity.

Nearby Attractions

Hartshill Hayes Country Park (SK 316944), a few miles south of Mancetter, can be reached by a pleasant walk along the canal towpath and across fields. The park is a marvellous open area with wide ranging views. Two nature trails can be followed through woodland which is rich in bird life.

Rambles around the woodland of Monks Park and Bentley Park, a few miles south-west, are recommended, particularly on a spring morning when the dawn chorus is unforgettable. Although the woods are private, they are crossed by public footpaths and bridleways.

The Trail

1. This Trail is very much like a football match – in two halves. The first part wanders through the older part and along the tranquil Coventry Canal. The second half, which returns through the modern corner, is quite pleasant but cannot match the first delightful mile, so you'll be forgiven if you take the option of returning along the towpath. The Trail starts from St Peter's Church. There has probably been a place of worship on this site since the 10th century and the unassuming building seen today dates from the early 13th. The stained glass is of particular interest and the east window is thought to have been part of the Jesse window from nearby Merevale Abbey. The key can be obtained from the Vicarage in Quarry Lane. The row of black and white houses by the church and the group across the road, fronted by a Gothic veranda, are almshouses which were built in 1728 funded by an endowment by James Gramer, a London goldsmith who came from Atherstone. Walk through the churchyard and past the almshouses on the right and turn right up Quarry Lane.

18th century almshouses, Mancetter

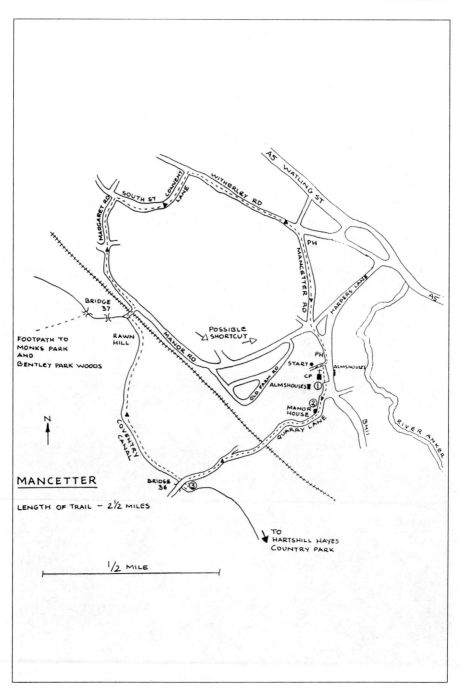

MANCETTER

LENGTH OF TRAIL — 2½ MILES

2. On the corner is the magnificent early 14th century timbered Manor House with gazebos on each corner. Previous inhabitants were the three Glover brothers who, during the reign of Mary Tudor, were active Protestants and were eventually arrested. One of the brothers, Robert was burnt at the stake and became known as the Mancetter Martyr. A little further on is the 18th century Manor House Farm. The neighbouring timber-framed barn has been recently renovated and is now a separate property. The lane soon emerges into open countryside and care is needed as there is no pavement. Go over the railway bridge and continue down the lane to reach the Coventry Canal which runs from Coventry to Fradley and was completed in 1790.

3. Go down the slope and turn right along the towpath under bridge 36. (A very enjoyable walk goes left along the towpath and then across fields to Hartshill Hayes Country Park). Follow the towpath as it winds through the countryside with lush wooded areas on the opposite bank. Birdlife abounds and if you're lucky you may see Sparrowhawks displaying over the woods. The towpath circles around Rawn Hill on the opposite bank and just before the next bridge (37), where the canal runs parallel with the railway, turn right over a metal bridge. (As mentioned earlier, this is the spot where you can beat a retreat along the towpath if you wish). If not, follow the lane to the right to the main road.

4. (A short cut back to the start is possible by turning right, but the estate you would pass through is not pleasant). It's far better to turn left along Margaret Road, where the short section between factories soon leads to a pleasant suburb. At a junction, turn right down South Street and right again down Convent Lane. At a T-junction, turn right along Witherley Road and after about half a mile, take the right fork in the road by the Blue Boar Inn, along Mancetter Road. This leads to a junction of roads by the post office where a right turn leads to The Plough Inn which is a popular hostelry with a varied menu. The church and the start are beyond this pub.

Napton on the Hill

Access

Napton on the Hill (SP 465611 – OS Landranger 151) is perched above the A425, between Southam and Daventry. Buses regularly call here from Leamington, Southam and Rugby. Parking is possible by the church but not during a service.

The Village

Napton on the Hill is aptly named as it developed on the slopes of the 452 feet hill which bears its name and from which I'm told keen eyes can see seven counties. The village was already a settlement of considerable importance by 1086. It was granted a weekly market and

Napton Locks

annual fair in 1321 and prospered during the Middle Ages, becoming one of the largest towns in the county. Neither the market nor the fair continue today.

On the approach roads to Napton, the village's situation on a hill would be striking enough in this flat countryside but the prominent landmarks of the windmill and church draw the eye for miles around. The church stands sentinel on a superb hilltop site as a reminder of the village's past status. Alongside the canal to the north of the village is a small industrial estate, once the site of Napton Brick and Tile Works.

Nearby Attractions

Napton is surrounded by excellent walking country. Paths along the Oxford Canal and over the hills and woodland of Shuckburgh Park are all enjoyable, easily accessible routes. The Oxford Canal was engineered by James Brindley and follows the natural contours of the countryside, unlike a "cut" canal such as the Grand Union which slices through natural barriers.

Napton Reservoir (SP 467626) was originally constructed to maintain the water levels in both the Oxford and Grand Union canals and now provides a valuable haven for many water birds, including the reed bunting, a striking bird with distinctive head markings.

The Trail

1. The Trail starts from the church. On the noticeboard outside, there is a leaflet about the village nature trail, which in four miles follows paths to the canal and reservoir. The Norman church of St Lawrence has an interesting story attached to its construction. The church was supposed to be built at the foot of the hill but the stones were mysteriously moved to the hilltop overnight. Not by the devil, who was apparently causing trouble elsewhere, but by fairies. Those villagers who make the long climb each Sunday may regret this piece of mischief. The north door, known as the Devil's door, got its name when the door was opened during a Baptism to allow the Devil to escape. A very curious feature is the vestry door adorned with a hatch and grille. At the base of the chancel arch can be seen an ancient carved head, part of an

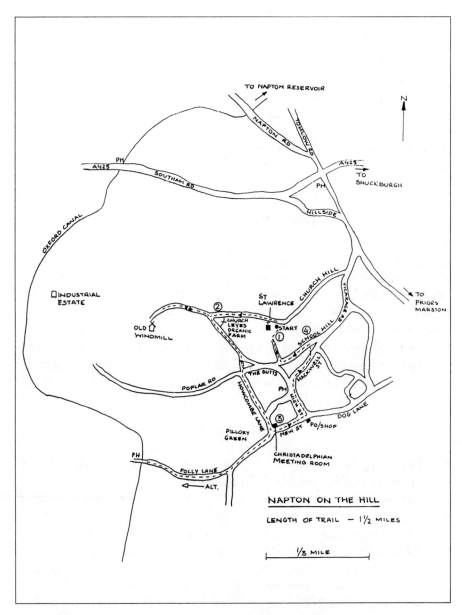

TO NAPTON RESERVOIR

N

A425

PH

SOUTHAM RD

A425

TO
SHUCKBURGH

PH

HILLSIDE

OXFORD CANAL

CHURCH HILL

TO
PRIORS
MARSTON

☐ INDUSTRIAL
ESTATE

ST
LAWRENCE

VICARAGE RD

OLD ☐
WINDMILL

CHURCH
LEYES
ORGANIC
FARM

■ ●START
①

②

④

SCHOOL HILL

POPLAR RD

THE BUTTS

HOWCOMBE LANE

HIGH ST

HACKWELL ST

PH

③

NEW ST

PO/SHOP

DOG LANE

PILLORY
GREEN

PH

FOLLY LANE

CHRISTADELPHIAN
MEETING ROOM

◄—ALT.

NAPTON ON THE HILL

LENGTH OF TRAIL — 1 ½ MILES

⊢——— ⅓ MILE ———⊣

older Norman wall upon which the arch was built. The church
was restored during Victorian times by the Shuckburghs, a local
family from nearby Shuckburgh Hall.

2. With the church to the left, walk down the lane past Church Leyes organic farm, which is open every day except Saturday. To catch a glimpse of the windmill, continue ahead at the road junction but please remember that this is now a private house. Old maps show the presence of two mills close together, and records of a mill can be traced back to 1543. Retrace your steps to the junction, walk downhill and take the right fork to a crossroads. Walk ahead down Howcombe Lane passing the Christadelphian meeting room on Pillory Green at the end. (From here, a pleasant walk goes right and at the next junction right again to the Oxford Canal and The Folly pub. There can be few more enjoyable ways of watching the world go by than from a canal towpath and this section is very popular with pleasure boats, walkers and cyclists).

3. Turn left past the post office and village stores and at the next junction, bear left up the High Street passing The Crown pub. Bear right into Hackwell Street (pavement on the left). A considerable amount of renovation work on old houses and haphazard modern development has resulted in a hotch-potch of styles, some of which stick out like a sore thumb. Just past a house with a wooden upper storey, turn left up steep steps, emerging onto School Hill.

4. Turn left past more new houses, and when you reach a small green by The Butts, turn right and climb steeply up an alleyway passing the Payne Light, a lamppost erected in memory of a Napton headmaster. At the top of the hill, after a steady plod and with some relief, you will reach the churchyard and the start.

Offchurch

Access

Offchurch (SP 360656 – OS Landranger 151) can be found just off the Fosse Way (B4455), 3 miles east of Leamington Spa. Street parking is possible with care by the church. Good bus connections to Leamington, Southam and Rugby.

St Gregory's church

The Village

Offchurch, a settlement since Saxon times, has a long and fascinating history including a connection with Offa, the Saxon King of Mercia. The story goes that the church of St Gregory was built by Offa in memory of his son, Fremund, who was murdered nearby. Little did this Saxon King realise he would become more famous for a long distance footpath than for his kingly exploits! Little of the original Saxon church remains. Offa was also responsible for building a hunting lodge and the site is now occupied by a 19th century house, Offchurch

Bury. Excavations in 1866 revealed an ancient burial ground on the site of the church when weapons and jewellery were unearthed dating back to 650 AD. In the 11th century, the manor belonged to Leofric, Earl of Mercia and husband of Lady Godiva, otherwise known as Coventry's first streaker.

The Village of black and white half timbered and thatched cottages together with red brick houses enjoys attractive views south. Natural and man made boundaries surround the village giving it an isolated, secluded feel. To the north is the River Leam; to the south runs the Grand Union Canal; the ancient drovers' road known as the Welsh Road passes through the parish and to the east is the old Roman road, the Fosse Way, now a fast modern highway. This runs almost parallel to a dismantled railway, and the section south of Offchurch is still fairly well preserved.

Nearby Attractions

Many charming walks are possible around Offchurch, across the parkland of Offchurch Bury to Newbold Comyn Park. Paths linking Cubbington, Hunningham and Weston under Wetherley to the north are also worth exploring.

The Grand Union Canal passes through countryside to the south of Offchurch and is a valuable refuge for wildlife in this intensively farmed landscape. A walk along the towpath into Leamington Spa is recommended.

The Trail

1. The Trail, which does have a couple of stiles to climb, starts at the bus stop at the junction by the church. Facing the bus stop, turn left, signed to Long Itchington. Walk past red brick houses with attractive gardens and just past the last house on the left, go over a stile on the left into a field. Keep the hedge on the left to the bottom corner of the field. Fine open views across this fertile landscape can be enjoyed as you descend.

2. Go over the stile in the corner and emerge onto the road by Nine Hills Cottage. Turn left along the road, (no pavement for a short

distance) past a junction and then join the pavement on the right
and walk into the village.

3. You will shortly reach a road junction by the thatched Stag's Head
    which offers a good selection of food and drink. This area around
    the pub with its mix of modern brick houses and black and white
    half timbered cottages is attractive, especially in summer when
    gardens are in full bloom. Just past the pub, turn left up the hill
    to reach the church at the top and the start.

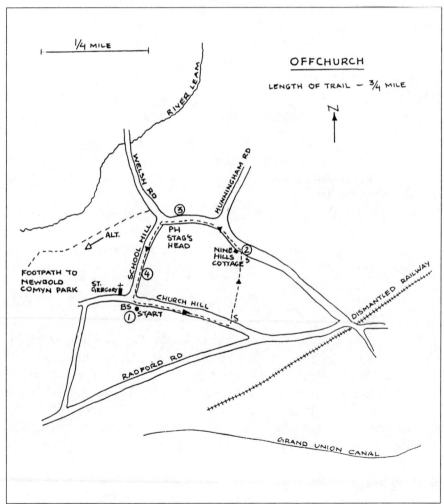

4. The churchyard of St Gregory's is part of the Living Churchyard
Scheme whereby areas are left unmown during the summer to
encourage the growth of wildflowers, which consequently attract
insects and birds. Much of the present church is of Norman
origin, built in the 12th century and the interior is of great
interest. What is claimed to be the coffin of King Offa can be seen;
this was originally found under the porch. Presumably there is a
piece missing or else Offa was extremely small! Stone from the
coffin lid is said to be built into the north wall, but this is difficult
to spot. You will also notice that the nave walls bulge outwards,
because the original roof was too heavy. Scattered about the
church are information boards which, together with a fascinating
church guide, supply further interesting snippets of history.
Outside on the tower are pockmarks said to be the marks of shots
fired by Cromwell's soldiers. Fresh from a skirmish, they obviously felt the need for more target practice and picked on the
church tower. Another story attached to the church is that of a
resident ghost. In the 17th century, a man was murdered outside
the church, but his murderer was never caught and it is said that
the victim's ghost wanders the churchyard searching for his
assailant.

Polesworth

Access

Polesworth (SK 264025 – OS Landranger 140) is located off the A5, 3 miles east of Tamworth. The railway station is at the north end of the village and Polesworth has a regular bus service to Birmingham, Nuneaton and Tamworth. Free parking is available off the main street by the library.

The Village

Polesworth lies at the northern end of Warwickshire in a valley by the river Anker. The name comes from "Pol" meaning deep water and "Worth" meaning dwelling. With its streets of terraced houses, it is

The vicarage, Polesworth

far from being a picturesque village but the visitor will nevertheless find much of historical interest, and there remains a surprising amount of open space, particularly around the old Abbey Green near the river.

Polesworth has a long history as a mining village and was one of the first communities to enjoy the benefits of electricity, generated by its own colliery at Pooley Hall. The river Anker was once diverted to facilitate the coal mining operations but it now follows its original course. The Coventry Canal also cuts through the village on the southern side. The older part of the village has connections with King Alfred; a nunnery, dedicated to his daughter Editha, was founded here in 827. The nearby manor house of Pooley Hall was built by Thomas Cockayne in 1507.

Nearby Attractions

Alvecote Pools (SK 253040), a few miles north, is a slowly maturing nature reserve managed by the Warwickshire Wildlife Trust. It was once a colliery site which closed in 1965, and nature is gradually reclaiming the land. As one of a string of wetland sites in the Midlands, it is a valuable stopping point for birds during spring and autumn migrations. Birds which have been seen include great crested grebe, pochard, tufted duck, snipe, redshank and little ringed plover.

The ruins of Alvecote Priory (SK 251043) next to the Pools, mark the site of a small Benedictine priory, said to have been established by William Burdett as a penance for killing his wife after rumours of her infidelity. Rumours which later proved unfounded. Little remains except a moulded doorway and a dovecote and the site is now a peaceful picnic area from which walks can be enjoyed along the towpath of the Coventry Canal.

The Trail

1. The Trail starts from the car park. Turn left out of the car park, opposite the Red Lion pub and walk down Bridge Street past shops and across the bridge over the River Anker. During spring, mute swans take advantage of the lack of disturbance to nest on

the floating island in the centre of the river, and the downy cygnets are a delight. Walk past the bus stop and turn right at the crossroads down Tamworth Road to the canal bridge.

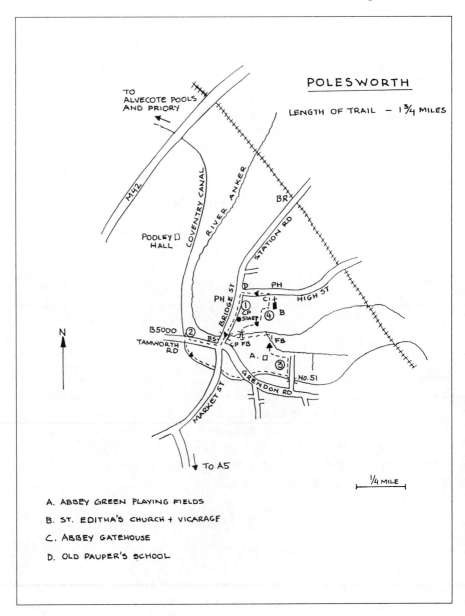

A. ABBEY GREEN PLAYING FIELDS

B. ST. EDITHA'S CHURCH + VICARAGE

C. ABBEY GATEHOUSE

D. OLD PAUPER'S SCHOOL

2. Turn right to reach the towpath and then left under the bridge and along the towpath. With derelict buildings backing onto the water, this is not the most attractive canal section in Warwickshire but with luck and keen eyes, the quiet walker may see plenty of birdlife, including wagtails and occasionally, during the summer, terns patrolling the water for food. Walk under two bridges and at the third (number 51), leave the towpath and turn left onto playing fields. This park was once the site of Park Farm which was used during World War II for open-cast coal mining but after the war, it was returned to the villagers who transformed it into this valuable open space.

3. Bear left past the football field on a tarmac path and, level with a building, turn right on the path to the river. On the way, you will pass overgrown ditches where the river was diverted from its original course. Now abandoned, the reed filled water provides a marvellous habitat and nature lovers will be rewarded with the sound of sedge warblers in summer, singing in a most unlikely setting. The path leads over a footbridge and alongside the river with charming views to the church on the far side. After reaching a car park, turn right over two more bridges across the river. The old bridge, crossed earlier, can be seen more clearly. Keep ahead on the paved path and at the end, take the first path on the right alongside a field.

4. This becomes enclosed between hedges and emerges by the church and half timbered vicarage, built in 1868. St Editha's Abbey Church is all that remains of a much larger abbey complex. Turn left past the memorial cross and under the 15th century Abbey gatehouse which has been significantly altered through the years. Turn left along the High Street and at the corner, note the building on the right. Now used as a nursery, the inscription over the door records its use as a Paupers' School for boys and girls, rebuilt in 1818. Turn left down Bridge Street to reach the start.

Priors Marston

Access

Priors Marston (SP 490575 – OS Landranger 151) hides among a tangle of minor roads, reached either off the A361, A423 or A425. Very limited parking in Vicarage Lane or School Lane near the church. Buses to Banbury only on Thursdays.

The Village

Priors Marston is a delectable, tranquil village, set snugly beneath the edge of the neighbouring Northamptonshire uplands. This secluded corner is rarely visited although it is one of the most interesting and

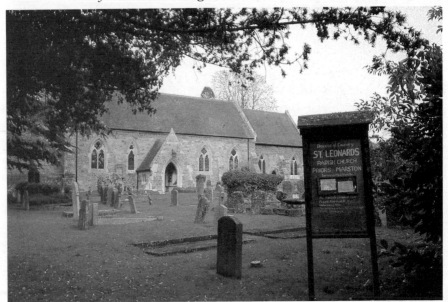

St Leonard's church

picturesque villages in Warwickshire. Records of a settlement on this site date back over a thousand years. Both this and nearby Priors Hardwick were originally held by the Priors of Coventry in the 11th century but after the Dissolution passed to the Spencer family, who are still Lords of the Manor.

The Village is surrounded by trading routes both old and new which testify to the wealth of history in this area. The Welsh Drovers Road runs through the parish to the south; this was used to drive sheep to market in London from the Welsh borders, thus avoiding the main toll roads. The Oxford Canal winds through the countryside to the west and the old Jurassic Way and an ancient Salt Road running from Droitwich to Northampton also pass through the parish.

Nearby Attractions

Across the Northamptonshire border to the east can be found the attractive villages of Hellidon and the Catesbys. This hilly countryside is well worth exploring and there are delightful walks through Fawsley Park and Badby Woods.

A pleasant ramble leads west across fields to the village of Priors Hardwick with its interesting church and popular pub.

The Trail

1. The Trail starts by the church. (Later, there are a couple of stiles to climb and a little mud to negotiate but nothing difficult). The 13th century St Leonard's Church stands in a particularly serene setting at the heart of the village and has seen extensive changes through the years. One unusual feature is the vivid stained glass in the porch and the plaque on the floor in memory of Richard West. It was believed to be a form of humility to be buried in the porch so that those entering would walk over you. Why the Wests sought this humility is not clear. Modern stained glass installed in 1993 may not please everyone but it's certainly a distinctive style and full of colour. Tucked away on a window sill near the altar is a 14th century cross, recently recovered from a nearby garden. Inside, are interesting leaflets on the history of the church and village. Walk through the churchyard which is dominated by two magnificent cedar trees, almost 200 years old. In summer,

with luck, you may see the spotted flycatchers which nest in the churchyard. From the porch, take the path on the right and go out onto School Lane.

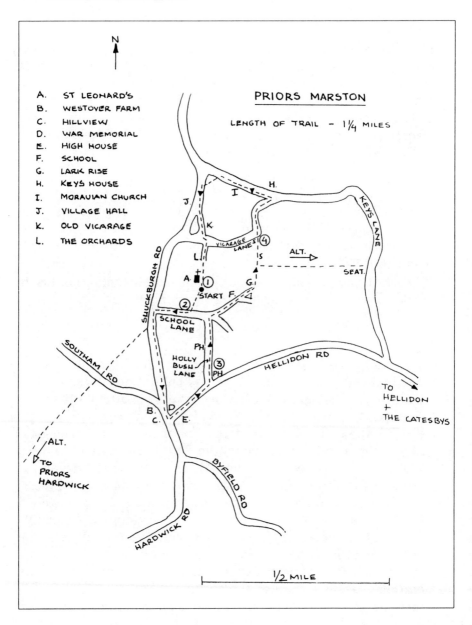

2. Turn right and at the T-junction, left down Shuckburgh Road. At the end, pass Westover Farm and Hillview to reach The Green with its war memorial. Edward Gardiner, a famous craftsman who made Gimson chairs, lived and worked in Hillview House until his death in 1958. Fortunately the craft survives elsewhere and Gimson chairs are still made today. Turn left up Hellidon Road passing the 200 year old High House. Note the small castellated building on the right, a boiler house to an adjacent, but no longer extant, kitchen garden and greenhouses. Turn left along Holly Bush Lane passing the Falcon pub. Although there has been a pub on this site since 1480, the current building dates from the 17th century.

3. From here, you will be following the blue (not yellow) brick road, or rather path. This was paid for by Mr Ted Masters so he could walk to the Moravian church without getting his shoes dirty – an expensive way to keep your shoes clean. You also pass the site of the original Methodist Chapel, now a private house. Go past The Holly Bush Inn, granted a full licence only in 1947. Before then, 100 years ago, it was a shop selling beer. A forge and wheelwright's shop once occupied the site of the car park. At the next junction, turn right up School Lane. Take the left fork and pass the school which has been here since 1849. Walk up the drive of Lark Rise and go through a gate on the left onto a footpath. (The path which shortly branches right up the hill is worth following for the splendid views). Continue ahead, over a stile and up the alleyway, crossing another stile at the far end. The upside down footpath sign must be an Australian import!

4. Turn right and follow the road as it bends left, then right and eventually turn left along Keys Lane. Keys House opposite was the home of Josiah Key who, in 1711, founded a local education charity. Walk past the Moravian church, opened in 1862, and opposite the next junction, by a no cycling sign, turn left down an alleyway which emerges onto Shuckburgh Road. Turn left passing the Village Hall on the opposite side and three cottages on the left. Bear left, still on the blue brick road, past the Old Vicarage to reach Vicarage Lane. Head past The Orchards, lovely cottages with beautiful gardens to reach the church and the start.

Ratley

Access

Ratley (SP 383473 – OS Landranger 151) is perched on top of Edge Hill and accessible from the A422 or the B4086. Parking is possible by the village hall on Town Hill. Limited bus service to Tysoe from where a sporadic service runs to Shipston or Stratford.

The Village

Ratley is a compact, secluded village gathered around a series of terraces and horseshoe-shaped lanes leading to a small green. The mellow Hornton stone cottages stand higgledy-piggledy at all angles yet blend together in surprising harmony. Ratley also stands on the main watershed between the Severn and the Thames. The lie of the land leaves little room for expansion in the lower part of the village and new houses are confined to the top road towards Edge Hill. The village was recognised in 1971 as a Conservation Area which has

12th century preaching cross,
St Peter ad Vincula church

helped preserve its character. As in many other villages, Ratley no longer has a school so local children must travel to Tysoe.

To the north-east there is evidence of a settlement going back to the Iron Age and excavations on Nadbury Camp, now divided by a busy road, have revealed weaponry and skeletons. In the troubled times of the Civil War, many Warwickshire villages were affected and Ratley, standing so close to Edge Hill, was inevitably caught up in the aftermath of the battle. Many casualties were buried in a mass grave behind the church.

Nearby Attractions

Reached by a pleasant walk is Edge Hill (SP 375475), where, on 23rd October 1642, the Civil War began with the first, inconclusive battle between Royalists and Parliamentarians. At the time, the hilltop was bare of trees. The beeches were planted in the 18th century to mark the position of the Royalist army. Give your imagination full rein and picture the scene as the opposing armies massed to do battle. The actual site of the encounter is away to the north on inaccessible MOD land, but this wonderful viewpoint has become the accepted place of pilgrimage. The popular yet rather peculiar structure, the Castle Inn, built around 1750 by Sanderson Miller, is supposed to mark the spot where Charles I raised his standard before the battle.

Radway village (SP 370481) nestles at the foot of Edge Hill and can be reached via a steep path from the Castle Inn. Unrivalled views are ample recompense for the effort.

The Trail

1. The Trail starts from the village hall. From the car park, turn left up Town Hill where the road runs high above a road down on the left. At the junction, turn sharp left onto this sunken road, the High Street. This passes an old drinking trough and bends left into Church Street. From here, look back to the left of a magnificent copper beech. The mound on the hill is the only visible remains of the castle earthworks, but it stands on private land. The castle is thought to date back to 1140. Built by Hugh de Arden, it fell into decay by the 13th century and was excavated in the late 1960s.

2. Continue along Church Street, passing a plaque on the wall commemorating this building as The First Post Office, with an old post-box in the wall. This was once the general store which sold just about everything. You will soon reach the church, the heart of this small community.

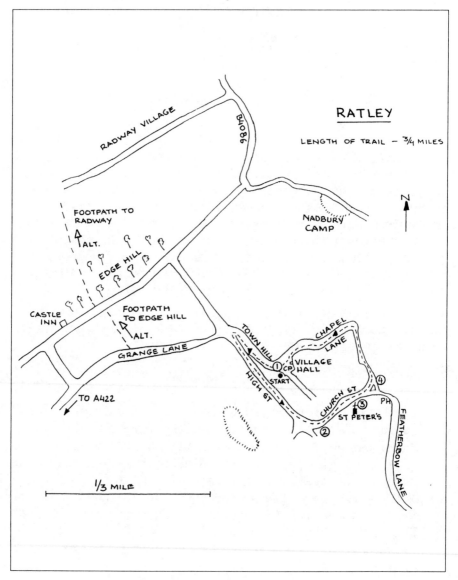

3. The 13th century St Peter's Church, built of local stone, has a large stone and marble reredos. An unusual feature is the lack of capitals on top of the arch pillars. Brass tablets on the west wall commemorate the Lewis family who owned a considerable amount of property in the area. In the churchyard is a mediaeval preaching cross dating back to the 13th century. The trough by the main gate was used for salting pork. The grooves in the outside wall nearest the pulpit are said to be from sharpening arrow heads, and this may also explain the name of the lane by the green: Featherbow Lane. This dates from the time when archery was practised in churchyards and when archers were an invaluable element in the army.

4. Walk past the church to the small village green on Featherbow Lane, with the Rose & Crown pub on the right. This listed building offers a good selection of food and drink, and boasts the obligatory ghost. The bar is said to be haunted by the spirit of a Civil War soldier who hid up the chimney. (We meet another ghost with a chimney fetish at Warmington). Walk left of the green and bear left into Chapel Lane. This climbs and bears left, passing an old chapel to reach the village hall and the start.

Royal Leamington Spa

Access

R oyal Leamington Spa (SP 319656 – OS Landranger 151), 2 miles east of Warwick, is reached either off the A445 or the A425. Good train and bus services connect with Coventry, Warwick, Stratford, Kenilworth and Rugby as well as more remote villages, many featured in this book. Ample parking is well signposted. An excellent base for touring, there is a good choice of accommodation.

The Town

Leamington Spa is a graceful, genteel town, full of character and free of the hordes that descend on Warwick and Stratford. Fine Regency buildings, elegant terraces and squares make Leamington a joy to

Regency houses, Lansdowne Crescent

walk around. Lansdowne Crescent, Newbold Terrace and Clarendon Square are especially attractive and opulent examples of Regency architecture. The river Leam winds its stately progress through the town, its banks blessed with immaculate, colourful parks and gardens.

Mineral springs have been used since Elizabethan times but it was not until 1784, when a new spring was discovered by two local men, Benjamin Satchwell and William Abbotts and the first spa baths built two years later, that Leamington developed as prosperously as Buxton, Matlock and Bath. Leamington has played host to many royal visitors through the years; the Prince Regent in 1819 and the young Princess Victoria in 1830. It can even boast its own world boxing champion.

Nearby Attractions

Newbold Comyn Park (SP 337655), on the outskirts of Leamington, offers play areas and nature trails together with riverside walks and marvellous views over the surrounding countryside.

The Grand Union Canal runs through Leamington and a delightful walk heads east towards Bascote Locks.

The Trail

1. The Trail starts outside the entrance to the Jephson Gardens by the Tourist Information Centre. To the left over Victoria Bridge is All Saints. This church of cathedral-like proportions replaced an earlier, much smaller, building. The interior is far more rewarding than the rather grim Victorian exterior and contains a remarkable variety of stained glass plus an intricately carved reredos depicting the Last Supper, based on a painting by da Vinci. In the adjoining chapel can be seen an exquisite triptych behind the altar. The great rose and wheel windows are of plain glass; what a sight they would be in vivid, patterned colour. Outside the main entrance is a stone, with a faded inscription, marking the site of the original mineral spring. To start the Trail, cross the road and walk to the right of The Assembly Rooms opposite. Go past the Pump Room, built in 1814 and frequented during the 1830s when Leamington was one of the most fashion-

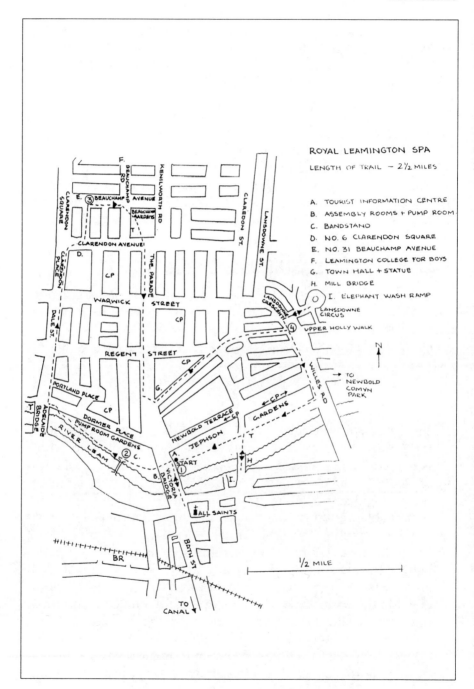

ROYAL LEAMINGTON SPA

LENGTH OF TRAIL — 2½ MILES

A. TOURIST INFORMATION CENTRE
B. ASSEMBLY ROOMS + PUMP ROOM
C. BANDSTAND
D. NO. 6 CLARENDON SQUARE
E. NO. 31 BEAUCHAMP AVENUE
F. LEAMINGTON COLLEGE FOR BOYS
G. TOWN HALL + STATUE
H. MILL BRIDGE
I. ELEPHANT WASH RAMP

able health resorts in England. By the 1840s, this fashion declined and the Pump Room has since changed hands several times. In the 1950s, extensive renovation was carried out and it reopened as a medical centre but this closed in 1990 and both this and the Assembly Rooms are to be refurbished to house an art gallery and museum.

2. Walk through the gardens, past the bandstand and bridge, keeping the River Leam on the left. Leave the gardens and turn left along Dormer Place. Turn right up Dale Street, cross over Portland Place, Regent Street and Warwick Street, all boasting excellent examples of Regency architecture. Continue ahead up Clarendon Place and turn right into Clarendon Square. As you pass No. 6, note the plaque commemorating Napoleon III, who spent part of his exile here. Turn left past the gardens to reach leafy Beauchamp Avenue, where No. 31 opposite is a beautiful example of the Regency style.

3. Turn right along Beauchamp Avenue and as you cross Beauchamp Road, note the Leamington College for Boys on the left, an impressive Victorian building in the Tudor style. Reach Beauchamp Gardens by the tennis courts, bear right across the gardens to The Parade, now the main shopping street but once a terrace of houses. Walk down The Parade over Warwick Street and past the Town Hall. The statue of Queen Victoria outside was definitely not amused in 1940 when a German bomb rocked her, literally, on her pedestal. Inside the Town Hall is a plaque in memory of Randolph Turpin who, in 1951, became world middleweight boxing champion when he beat Sugar Ray Robinson. Turn left up Regent Grove past a roundabout and over Clarendon Street to the junction with Willes Road.

4. A short detour left and then first right will reveal the elegant Lansdowne Crescent and Lansdowne Circus. The American author, Nathaniel Hawthorne lived at 10, Lansdowne Circus for a while. Return to Willes road and walk left (south) past the end of Newbold Terrace and cross to enter Jephson Gardens, dedicated in 1846 as a memorial to Dr Henry Jephson, who treated patients with the spa waters and helped make the town famous.

The original gift of land for the gardens however, was made by Edward Willes, a member of an influential local family. The gardens continue to delight both residents and visitors alike. Walk through the gardens with the river on the left to a main crossing path by the toilets. Follow the path on the left for a short detour to Mill Bridge, a suspension bridge opened in 1903, from which you can see the end of a cobbled ramp opposite which was an Elephant Wash Ramp. The mind boggles at the thought of elephants in the heart of elegant Leamington! It was used to bathe circus animals. Not quite an African watering hole but a bizarre sight nevertheless. Retrace your steps to the toilets and turn left to the main entrance and the start.

Rugby

Access

R ugby (SP 504752 – OS Landranger 140), is easily accessible from the M1/M6/M45 via the A426, A428 or A45, and has ample parking. National Express coaches call and this is a major British Rail junction. An excellent bus service connects with much of Warwickshire, including some of the villages in this book, making this an excellent base for a holiday.

The Town

Rugby, despite its modern, bustling centre, is a fascinating old market town with many buildings of considerable interest. In 1823, when William Webb Ellis of Rugby School picked up a football and ran with it, little did he realise he had just invented the game of rugby which would eventually make the town, and school, famous. Rugby also has connections with Thomas Hughes, author of "Tom Brown's Schooldays", a semi- autobiographical account of his time at the school. The poet, Rupert Brooke, once a master at the school, was born here.

The tourist information centre produces a detailed booklet on Rugby and the surrounding countryside. The town offers a bewildering choice of tea shops, pubs and restaurants, including perhaps the only McDonalds with a coat of arms above the door.

Nearby Attractions

East of Rugby is the Ashlawn Cutting Nature Reserve and Great Central Walk (SP 514746), on the line of a disused railway which once linked London and Nottingham. Cared for by the Warwickshire Wildlife Trust, the mixture of marsh, scrub and grassy banks is ideal for wildlife and shelters many rare plants.

Newbold on Avon nature reserve (SP 495767) is also managed by the Trust. The park occupies the site of a quarry which was worked for limestone until the 1920s and then flooded to form a pool, although one quarry face still towers over the water. Used until the 1980s as a top up reservoir for the neighbouring Oxford Canal, the park is now a valuable refuge for wildlife. The spoilheaps have been colonised by grassland, trees and scrub with the result that wildflowers and insects can be seen in abundance.

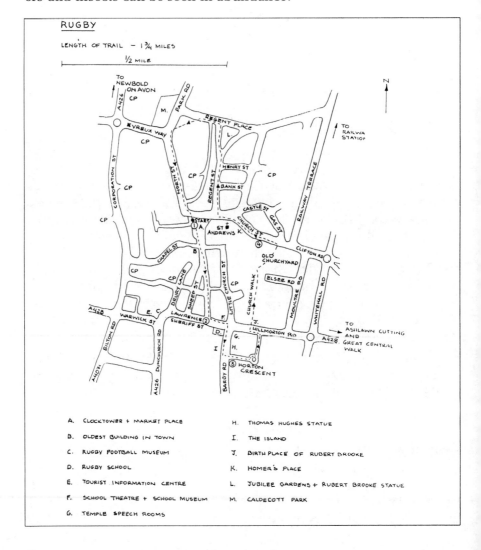

A. CLOCKTOWER + MARKET PLACE

B. OLDEST BUILDING IN TOWN

C. RUGBY FOOTBALL MUSEUM

D. RUGBY SCHOOL

E. TOURIST INFORMATION CENTRE

F. SCHOOL THEATRE + SCHOOL MUSEUM

G. TEMPLE SPEECH ROOMS

H. THOMAS HUGHES STATUE

I. THE ISLAND

J. BIRTHPLACE OF RUPERT BROOKE

K. HOMER'S PLACE

L. JUBILEE GARDENS + RUPERT BROOKE STATUE

M. CALDECOTT PARK

The Trail

1. The Trail starts from the Market Place by the clock tower, built in 1887 to celebrate Queen Victoria's Golden Jubilee. Although the Crown Hotel looks old, the timber frontage only dates from 1903. The view south down the High Street and Sheep Street reveals an interesting mix of building styles. Walk down the pedestrian precinct passing the end of Chapel Street, which contains the oldest building in the town, thought to be over 500 years old. Take the left fork into the High Street. When you reach Salter's shop, look for the barely dis-

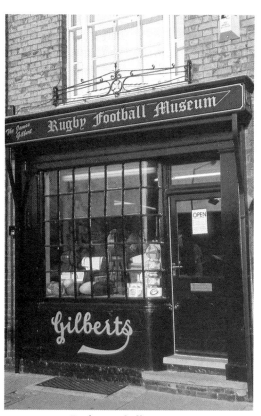

Rugby Football Museum

tinguishable fire mark between the first and second storeys. These marks are rarely seen today, but in the 18th century were essential because each insurance company's fire brigade would give priority to buildings bearing its own firemark. No fire mark – and presumably the building was allowed to burn down! At the end of High Street, enthusiasts of the game can visit the James Gilbert Rugby Football Museum to the right.

2. Turn left down Lawrence Sheriff Street, passing Rugby public school, which has a long and fascinating history, dating back to 1567. Details of school tours are available from the tourist office.

The architecture alone, mostly by Butterfield, is worthy of inspection. You also pass the L-shaped Headmaster's House with its octagonal tower. The building on the left is the School Theatre and in Little Church Street on the left is the School Museum. Turn right into Barby Road, on the corner of which is the Temple Speech Rooms, which serves as the school assembly hall and is named after Dr Frederick Temple, a former headmaster who later became Archbishop of Canterbury. Walk past School Close. On the left is a statue of Thomas Hughes and on the right is The Island, an ancient tumulus covered in trees, which until the 19th century had a moat and drawbridge. These defences came in handy when this was the scene of the great School Rebellion of 1797. The rioting pupils were eventually quelled by the militia and local farmers wielding horse whips – it's not known if this method is still used today to suppress unruly pupils.

3. Turn left into Horton Crescent and keep left until you reach Hillmorton Road where you turn left again. Turn right into Church Walk; Rupert Brooke was born in the corner house in 1887. He died, tragically young, during World War I, leaving a legacy of evocative poetry. Go past Elsee Road and towards the end of Church Walk, turn right to walk through the old churchyard of Holy Trinity. The church was demolished in the 1970s. The paved area by the park exit was the site of the Plaisance where there was once a ducking stool over a pond, used as a punishment for nagging wives – some husbands may regret its passing!

4. Turn left along Church Street, passing cobbled Homer's Place, where stands the former house of Count Wratislaw, reputedly a descendant of Good King Wenceslas. You will soon reach St Andrew's Church with its impressive tower, said to have been built with stone from the old castle. Turn right into Regent Street, where all the buildings, although of individual design, blend together surprisingly well. At the end, pass Jubilee Gardens with its statue of Rupert Brooke, and turn left along Regent Place. Keep left through Chestnut Field with Caldecott Park over to the right, and turn left along North Street to reach the Market Place and the start.

Shipston on Stour

Access

Shipston on Stour (SP 259405 – OS Landranger 151) is located on the A3400, 10 miles south of Stratford upon Avon. Good level of bus service to Stratford, Oxford, Banbury, Coventry and surrounding villages. Ample free parking in Mill Street by the bridge and off Telegraph Street.

The Town

Shipston on Stour, an attractive market town in the valley of the River Stour, was situated, until 1931, within Worcestershire. Its long and fascinating history dates back to the 8th century. The modern name derives from its old title of Sheep Wash Town, the "on Stour" was added to describe its position by the river. A charter for an annual fair and weekly market was granted in the 13th century. Its earlier fortunes were dependent on sheep and Shipston developed into a very prosperous wool town in the heart of the Feldon. This prosperity is reflected in the grand nature of the remaining buildings. Sheep Street, unsurprisingly, was the main commercial centre in the middle ages. Shipston was also on the line of busy coaching routes, and inns such as the George Hotel and White Bear, which survive to this day, developed into thriving hostelries.

Although the wool trade eventually declined, the town continued to flourish because it was served by a branch line of a 19th century tramway, the main line of which ran from Stratford to Moreton in Marsh. Today, Shipston is the main shopping area for many of the surrounding villages in Warwickshire, Oxfordshire and Gloucestershire. There is plenty of choice for refreshments with several pubs and, my usual downfall, teashops.

The Horseshoe

Nearby Attractions

An easy, pleasant walk leads south alongside the River Stour to the hamlet of Barcheston (SP 265399), where the church tower attempts to rival Pisa. Stand at the lychgate and you'll see its rather alarming list to port.

3 miles north is Honington (SP 266425), where attractive cottages in timber and stone cluster round a large village green. The five arch 17th century bridge and All Saints Church, containing several opulent monuments, are also worth a look. Honington Hall is open on Wednesdays from June to August.

The Trail

1. The Trail starts by Mill Bridge. There has been a bridge across the river since the 13th century although the current structure dates from 1826 when it was widened. With the bridge to the right, go left towards the one way system, and turn right up Church Street past the welcoming and attractive Horseshoe pub. Church Street is lined by many fine brick and timber framed

buildings from the 17th and 18th centuries. Walk past St Edmund's Church which has a 15th century west tower but a fairly ordinary interior. When you compare the magnificent edifice at Brailes, it's curious that the wealth generated by the wool trade didn't endow Shipston with a more opulent church. On the gable of a house can be seen an unusual windvane of an arrow piercing a crown, which was the emblem of St Edmund, a King of East Anglia.

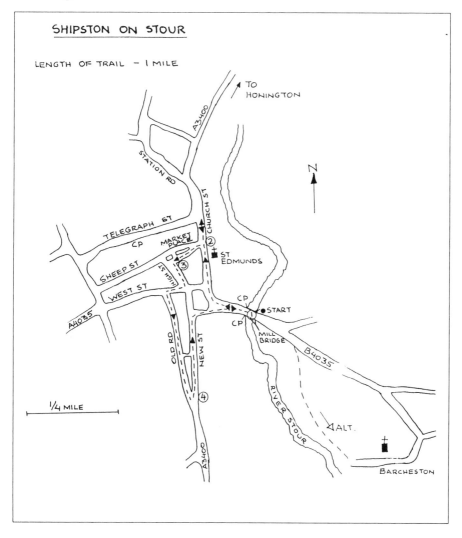

2. At the next corner, by the Market Place, the Trail goes left but it's worth continuing to see the attractive Georgian houses a little further on. Retrace your steps to the Market Place; on the corner is an interesting clock shop, Time in Hand. In the window is a remarkable example of Victorian engineering and ingenuity. Walk up the Market Place, taking the left fork along Sheep Street, an extremely handsome thoroughfare with stone, brick and stucco frontages. Turn left down the High Street.

3. This wide, elegant street was once the site of the market place. The George Hotel is an impressive Georgian brick building. At the end, turn right along West Street and shortly go left down Old Road, past the Methodist Church to the main road. The squat building on the left is the former National School for girls and infants. Notice the curious timber structure in the grounds of the building opposite.

4. Turn left up New Street, which is in fact older than Old Road, and just past the Coach & Horses you will reach the one way system. On closer inspection, the building ahead is revealed as a half timbered Indian restaurant. To reach the start, turn right to Mill Bridge.

Snitterfield

Access

S nitterfield (SP 218600 – OS Landranger 151) is accessible off the busy A46, 5 miles north-east of Stratford upon Avon. Bus services from Stratford, Warwick, Leamington, Kenilworth and Coventry call at the main square. Limited parking is possible by the church in Church Road.

The Village

Snitterfield, known as Snitfield in the 18th century, is a large village, bisected by the busy A46. Once visited by the Romans, Snitterfield developed in a clearing in the Forest of Arden, with an ancient road, the Marroway, passing nearby, heading for an old river crossing at Hampton Lucy. The houses are a mix of early Victorian and Georgian, together with the usual thatched, half timbered cottages and an attractive smattering of mellow brick farmhouses. You'll also notice many new red brick houses, usually described in the estate agent's blurb as "lux exec". For a long time the shop, as much the heart of any community as the church, was closed but has recently reopened.

However, it is for its connection with Shakespeare that Snitterfield is remembered. Shakespeare's grandfather Richard was a tenant farmer in the village and his son, John was born here around 1529. John eventually moved to Stratford where our Will was born but Richard's other son, Henry, the black sheep of the family, continued to live and farm in the village until his death in 1596. He is buried in the 14th century churchyard although the exact spot is unknown. Another less well known connection is with the Spencer family. A distant ancestor of the Princess of Wales was a John Spencer who lived in Snitterfield, but later moved to Wormleighton where he founded one of the most powerful mediaeval families in the land.

Nearby Attractions

Footpaths lead south from Snitterfield, across orchards and a golf course to the Welcombe Hills which were left to the people of Stratford by Flowers, the brewing family. The hills cover 70 acres of woods and grassland and offer wonderful walking, with extensive views over the Warwickshire plain. Welcombe Hills Obelisk is a striking landmark, 120 feet high. It was erected in 1876 to commemorate the Philips family, successful cotton manufacturers who built the mansion now occupied by the Welcombe Hotel.

The village of Wolverton, a few miles north, (SP 206624) is worth a visit, not least for its interesting church.

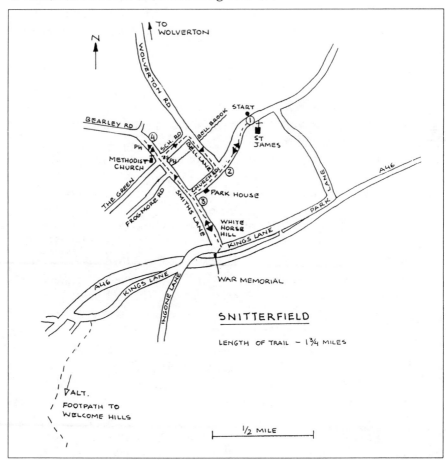

The Trail

1. The Trail starts from St James the Great Church which has an interesting interior, containing a decorated font, intriguing carved stall ends and monuments to the Philips family. The chancel arch is distorted, probably by the tremendous weight of the 15th century oak roof. The east window depicts four Bishops of Worcester: Egwin, Oswald, Dunstan and Wulstan. We have already visited the latter's birthplace at Long Itchington. The Black Death put a stop to all building work, leaving the tower unfinished and covered with thatch for many years. A former incumbent was Richard Jago, an eminent poet, who died here in 1781. Face the church and turn right along Church Road past some cottages. Mole End is quickly followed by Hare Cottage, after which you will pass a large house with a splendid wrought iron gateway above semi-circular stone steps.

2. Go past the end of Bell Lane and notice the magnificent old cedars on the left, once part of the Earls of Coventry's family estate. Snitterfield House, built by Thomas Coventry in 1668, was demolished in 1830, the only remains of this once grand estate being a garden wall, gateposts and Park House Cottages. Passing Elmdon House, watch out for the life-like owl on the gatepost. Reach the T-junction where the huge Park House is surmounted by a multitude of chimneys and an elaborate weathervane with a fox on top of a dome.

3. Turn left past the Londis shop along Smiths Lane which soon becomes White Horse Hill and at the T-junction, cross to the war memorial with its superb views. In the past, the vista would have encompassed the *Red* Horse on Sun Rising Hill above Middle Tysoe (featured in a later chapter), so why is this road *White* Horse Hill? Was there a White Horse nearby at some time? Don't breathe in too deeply though; the fumes come straight up from the A46 traffic, roaring past in a cutting a few feet below. Before this was built, the memorial occupied a quiet site between one part of the village and the other in King's Lane. Now the A46 has effectively cut King's Lane off from the rest of the village. It is claimed that this lane was used by Charles II in his flight from the Battle of

The school opened by Robert Philips MP

Worcester, although Charles seems to have had as many escape routes as Queen Anne had beds. Return to the junction by Londis and continue ahead past Frogmore Road to the square by The Foxhunter pub. Also surrounding the square are the Methodist Church and School founded in 1884 by the MP Robert Philips.

4. It's worth continuing to the Snitterfield Arms, which is an attraction not only for its food but also for the peculiar pub sign which depicts a bird, a snipe. At first glance, this seems an odd choice but there is a mundane explanation. In Anglo Saxon times, the village was known as Snytenfeld which apparently means "place of snipe", referring to the wet and marshy area around the brook, an ideal habitat for this distinctive bird. This land is now drained and the snipe have disappeared. Return to the junction and turn left down School Road which runs alongside Bell Brook. At the corner by a sign for a weak bridge, turn right up Bell Road and at the T-junction turn left along Church Road to the start.

Southam

Access

Southam (SP 419627 – OS Landranger 151) can be found off the A425, Leamington to Daventry road, and below the junction of the A423 and A426. In recent years, a bypass has reduced some of the town's traffic. A free car park with toilets is situated in Wood Street. Buses run to Leamington and Rugby.

The Town

Southam is a bustling, lively community which makes an excellent base to tour the area. The town was worthy of a mention in the Domesday book and testimony to earlier Roman occupation comes from the discovery of coins in the churchyard. Documentary evidence of a charter granted by King Ethelred the Unready giving Southam to Leofwine dates back to 998. In 1047, Southam passed to the Prior of Coventry. It was granted a market charter by Henry III in 1227 and has connections with Charles I, which we shall explore on the Trail. In August 1642, one of the first skirmishes of the Civil War, the Battle of Southam, took place at Southam Fields on the outskirts of the town.

Southam stands on the route of an ancient Welsh road, used by cattle drovers on their way to London and this traffic contributed to the town's prosperity and supported many coaching inns. Although the railway never reached Southam, the nationwide development of the "iron road" started the decline in the coaching trade during the 19th century. The town was also bypassed by the canal network. While not as elegant as other Warwickshire towns, there remains much to interest the visitor. Very few buildings pre-date the devastating fire of 1741 and much of the town was rebuilt in the Georgian style. Today, there is a great deal of modern development, while a battle is currently raging in an attempt to prevent the opening of a superstore on the bypass. The townsfolk quite rightly fear that it will take business away from the main street.

Holy Well near Southam

Nearby Attractions

Ufton Fields (SP 380615), cared for by the Warwickshire Wildlife Trust, is a fascinating nature reserve. The pools and limestone grassland encourage many birds and insects and there are two bird hides. Open to the public each Sunday and to Trust members at all times.

A pleasant walk leads west over fields to the Holy Well (SP 410618) whose origins are obscure. The intensely cold water is said to be a cure for eye ailments although experimenting isn't recommended. In 1925, the water was diverted to feed a reservoir and the spring dried almost to a trickle. Although no longer diverted, the general lowering of the water table means there is very little water in the well.

The Trail

1. The Trail starts from the car park in Wood Street. Turn right from the car park to the High Street. On the right is The Old Mint Inn squashed in the middle of a row of modern properties. The story goes that Charles I visited Southam following Edge Hill and commanded the local nobles to bring out all their silverware,

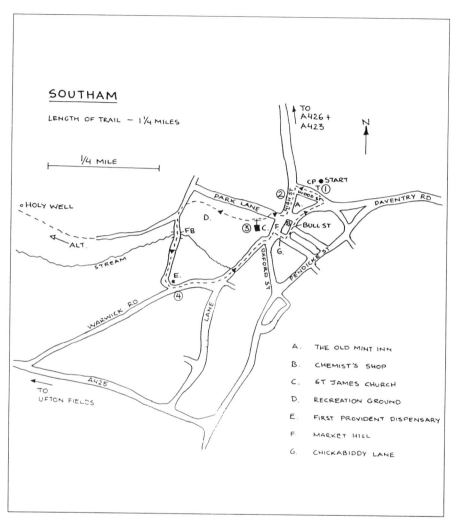

SOUTHAM

LENGTH OF TRAIL — 1¼ MILES

¼ MILE

TO
A426 +
A423

N

o HOLY WELL

PARK LANE

CP ● START

DAVENTRY RD.

ALT.

STREAM

FB

D.

BULL ST

WARWICK RD.

A425

TO
UFTON FIELDS

A. THE OLD MINT INN

B. CHEMIST'S SHOP

C. ST JAMES CHURCH

D. RECREATION GROUND

E. FIRST PROVIDENT DISPENSARY

F. MARKET HILL

G. CHICKABIDDY LANE

where it was minted into coins so that Charles could pay his soldiers, hence the inn's name. It is also claimed that the Old Mint is linked to the parish church by a secret tunnel. You will have to make do with the pedestrian crossing. The Old Mint Inn is a fascinating building in its own right. Built of stone with mullioned windows, it has been extensively restored but still retains some 16th century features and enough antique weaponry to start a minor battle.

2. Cross the High Street and turn left. On the opposite side of the road is a chemist's shop, which used to be the Manor House where Charles I may have slept. Turn right down Park Lane to go through the lychgate into the churchyard. The 14th century St James Church, built on the site of an earlier place of worship, was extensively restored in the 19th century. Of note is the 16th Century sandstone broach spire with four clock faces which towers 126 feet above the town. The lofty interior is impressive with carved angels on the stone supports to the roof beams and nave arches. There is an elaborately carved lectern and a rare coat of arms of Charles I, as well as the remains of Tudor lettering on the wall by the belfry screen. The Jacobean pulpit, lost for many years, was eventually rediscovered in a barn at Wormleighton. The churchyard contains graves commemorating the fallen of the Crimean War. Information boards around the church give details of many of the features.

3. Continue past the door and down the churchyard into the recreation ground. Aim for the top left corner of the field around the football pitch and through a gate. (The lane ahead joins the footpath to the Holy Well). Turn left over the footbridge and up an alleyway which eventually bears left to join the Warwick Road.

4. On the corner, is a stone memorial marking the site of the country's first provident dispensary, founded in 1823. Turn left past the hotel, passing imposing properties including The Abbey, which, as the name implies, stands on land once owned by the church. You will then reach the junction with the main street on Market Hill, site of the former cattle market, where you cross over and turn left. Soon, go right down the wonderfully named Chickabiddy Lane, part of an old poultry market site. At the end, turn left down Bull Street. Turn right at the end and just past the pub, take the first turning on the left back to the car park.

Stoneleigh

Access

Stoneleigh (SP 331726 – OS Landranger 140), 4 miles east of Kenilworth, is best reached off the A46. Parking is possible in a lay-by next to the bridge. A good bus service connects with Coventry, Leamington and Kenilworth. If the Royal Agricultural Show is on at the NAC, usually the first week in July, the area can be extremely congested.

The Village

Stoneleigh is an unspoilt estate village of great charm which has changed little and includes a pleasing collection of half timbered houses, cruck cottages and a splendid manor farmhouse. Once known as Stanlei, it was a royal manor with its own Hundred Court on Motslow Hill until the time of Henry I. The manor was later bestowed on the monks of Kenilworth until the Dissolution and in 1561 Sir Thomas Leigh, Lord Mayor of London, bought the estate. The village had a pub in the 19th century, The Stoneleigh Arms, but the riotous behaviour of some of the patrons so appalled Lord Leigh that he closed it down and decreed that there should never be another and that remains the case to this day. The former hostelry is now known as Forsythia Cottage.

To many, the name Stoneleigh conjures up the show ground where the famous Royal Agricultural Show is held each year. Stoneleigh Abbey nearby, whose 12th century Abbey buildings were established by Cistercian monks, has been incorporated into a Georgian mansion. The home of the Leigh family since the 16th century, this is the venue for the show as well as many other events and exhibitions throughout the year.

The Manor farmhouse

Nearby Attractions

A pleasant walk heads north alongside the river Sowe to Baginton (featured in an earlier chapter), which is also the nearest place for refreshments.

Ryton Pool (SP 375728), east of Stoneleigh, is a small lake adjoining a picnic area which was reclaimed from derelict land in the early 1980s. Shrubs and reeds are colonising the banks and birds have already discovered this vital refuge. An easy path leads round the pool.

The Trail

1. The Trail starts from the lay-by next to the 19th century eight arched bridge built by Rennie. Turn left over the bridge, crossing the road with great care (blind bends) and continue to a bend in the road opposite the bus stop. Again, cross with care to the green overlooked by a majestic horse chestnut, and walk down The Bank into The Green, where the Old Smithy stands, The date of 1851 can be seen on the far side.

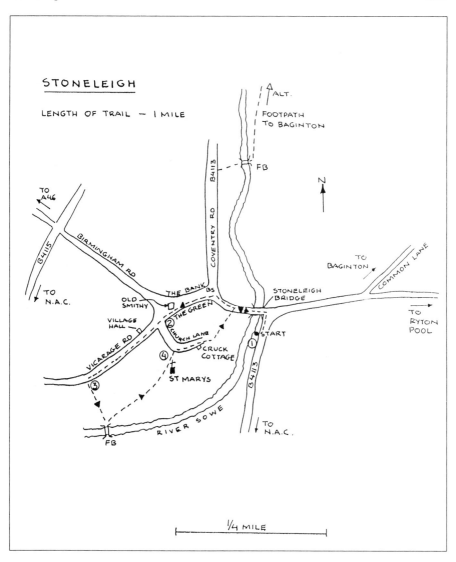

STONELEIGH

LENGTH OF TRAIL — I MILE

2. Bear left past the old almshouses. These were endowed in 1594 by Alice Leigh. Soon, you will walk past the Village Hall into Vicarage Road, passing an open field revealing pleasant views to the church. Pass by a beautiful, photogenic, black and white half timbered house; this dates from around the mid 16th century, although one wing was added in the 17th.

3. Opposite the drive to Holly House, turn left down a drive which leads to a bridge over the River Sowe. The causeway by the bridge comes in handy when the river floods, although on a summer's day, when the river level is low, it's hard to imagine it ever reaches this far up the lane. Before you come to the bridge, turn left through a gate and take the tarmac path to reach the church. St Mary's is 700 years old and much admired for its interior which includes a striking 17th century monument to Alice Leigh. Other items of interest are the box pews, an impressive wooden gallery, a magnificent Norman chancel arch and a font decorated with intricate carvings of the 12 apostles. It is said that this font originally came from Maxstoke Priory, elsewhere in Warwickshire. The tympanum is rather savage, depicting dragons and snakes biting their own tails. The pew cushions are covered in beautiful tapestry designs, all embroidered by villagers. However, you won't be able to take pictures of any of these features because photography is forbidden, an unusual ban for a Warwickshire church. Presumably, however, this doesn't apply to the exterior.

4. Leave the churchyard via a gate in the top left hand corner and turn right. Walk to the end of the lane passing Cruck Cottage and go through a gate at the end into a charming meadow. Follow the hedge on the left to a gate leading out onto the road by the bridge. Cross over and turn right over the bridge to reach the start.

Stratford upon Avon

Access

Stratford upon Avon (SP 206547 – OS Landranger 151) lies at the junction of the A46, A422, A439 and A3400. Ample parking is available; try and use the park and ride scheme off the Birmingham Road. An excellent bus service connects to much of Warwickshire, and the railway runs to Birmingham and Leamington. As you would expect, choice of accommodation is huge.

The Town

Much has been written about Stratford upon Avon's connection with William Shakespeare; the two remain forever linked in people's minds, although he spent a large part of his life in London. The influence of this our greatest writer pervades the town. Even if you dislike his work and insist "It's all Greek to me", by using this phrase, you are, however unwittingly, quoting Shakespeare. His legacy of plays, perennially topical and displaying a profound understanding of human nature, has bequeathed to us a treasure house of words and phrases which enrich our language. Hundreds, if not thousands, of books have been written about Shakespeare and anyone curious about every detail of his life, both real and speculative, is well catered for. Open all year, the Shakespeare properties are fascinating with superb gardens. A combined entry ticket is good value for money.

The original settlement grew up around a crossing point on the River Avon. In the 12th century, the Bishop of Worcester granted a market charter to the townsfolk and the town has prospered ever since. In 1996 the town celebrated its 800th year as a trading centre with the erection of a fountain in Bancroft Gardens. The street plan of parallel streets has altered little and would still be familiar to Shakespeare today, although he might raise an eyebrow at the proliferation of gift shops. If you have a choice, visit during midweek or out of season and walk everywhere. During the summer, Stratford suffers from considerable traffic congestion, while the hordes of visitors who "do" England in a week, seeing Stratford through a coach window, miss a great deal.

Nearby Attractions

Mary Arden's House in Wilmcote (SP 165584), 3 miles north and best reached by train, bus or along the canal towpath, was the home of Shakespeare's mother during her early years. There is a fascinating museum of country life, a dovecote and falconry.

Anne Hathaway's Cottage, Shottery (SP 185547), reached on foot across playing fields or by bus, was the childhood home of Shakespeare's wife. The colourful gardens are beautifully laid out and if you cross the road to Jubilee Gardens you'll see an unfamiliar, but charming view of the house.

Nash's House and gardens on the site of New Place

The Trail

1. The Trail starts from the Tourist Information Centre at Bridge-foot. Cross the road and go into Bancroft Gardens by the Gower Memorial. An impressive memorial to Shakespeare, this was erected by Lord Gower and unveiled in 1888. Strangely, the statue looks away from the river and presides over a depressing view of traffic and modern buildings. No wonder William's expression is disapproving. There are striking corner statues of Hamlet, Prince Hal, Macbeth and Falstaff and the statue is festooned with marvellous quotations from the plays. To the right of the memorial, use the pedestrian bridge to cross the river Avon. To the left you can see Clopton Bridge; the wooden original was replaced in the late 15th century by Sir Hugh Clopton. It demands a leap of the imagination to picture the old approach to this bridge across swampy meadows, a flood plain now drained and occupied by the Bancroft Gardens. Just beyond the end of the bridge is The Butterfly Farm. Open all year, it's home to various species of butterflies, moths and birds and an Insect City. As an arach-naphobe, I've never been brave enough to investigate but I'm told it houses some of the world's most dangerous spiders, which can be viewed in perfect safety. (The path beyond the Butterfly Farm leads onto the Tramway, the site of an old branch line running to Shipston on Stour. You can follow this path high above the recreation ground to join a path leading to the river. See the map for details).

2. Turn right and follow the path alongside the river, with a view across to the RSC theatre. This peaceful path hugs the riverbank past the bowling green, foot ferry and the Colin P. Witter Lock. The best view of the church is from the end of the lock; truly a photographer's delight, with the church framed by willow trees and reflected in the river. Walk past the weir and cross the river at the next footbridge. (The path continues alongside the river or by the road to The Greenway, an old railway line which is now a walkway and cycleway). Over the footbridge, turn right up an alleyway onto Mill Lane which leads to Holy Trinity Church. This glorious edifice stands in an idyllic setting overlooking the

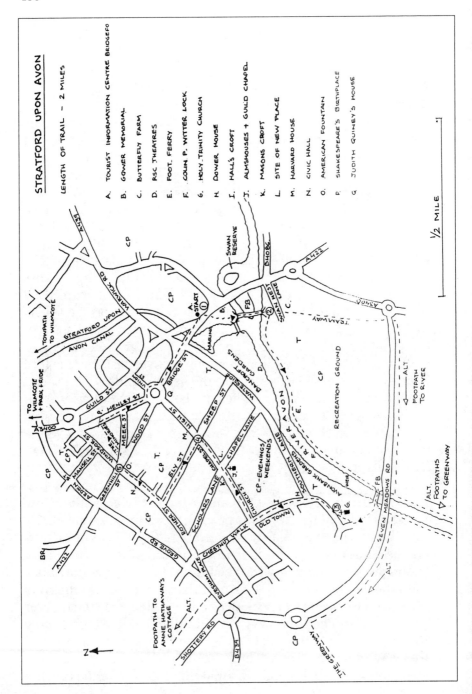

STRATFORD UPON AVON

LENGTH OF TRAIL – 2 MILES

A. TOURIST INFORMATION CENTRE BRIDGEFO
B. GOWER MEMORIAL
C. BUTTERFLY FARM
D. RSC THEATRES
E. FOOT. FERRY
F. COLIN P. WITTER LOCK
G. HOLY TRINITY CHURCH
H. DOWER HOUSE
I. HALL'S CROFT
J. ALMSHOUSES + GUILD CHAPEL
K. MASONS CROFT
L. SITE OF NEW PLACE
M. HARVARD HOUSE
N. CIVIC HALL
O. AMERICAN FOUNTAIN
P. SHAKESPEARE'S BIRTHPLACE
Q. JUDITH QUINEY'S HOUSE

½ MILE

Avon. Dating from the 13th Century, the interior has entertaining carved misericords and a beautiful east window. The rather garish bust of Shakespeare overlooks his grave in front of the altar, a "shrine" which attracts pilgrims from all over the world.

3. Turn right from the churchyard entrance, past the entrance to Avonbank Gardens (where another lovely riverside path leads to the theatre), and cross the end of Southern Lane. Continue past the Dower House through Old Town past Halls Croft, where Shakespeare's daughter, Susanna lived following her marriage to Dr John Hall. As well as an interesting exhibition, the visitor can enjoy an excellent tea room. Turn right up Church Street past Masons Croft, once the home of Marie Corelli, the eccentric 19th century novelist. Further along are 15th century almshouses, built by the Guild of the Holy Cross, still providing homes for elderly townsfolk to this day. The Guild Chapel beyond was founded in 1296. On the next corner in Chapel Street is the site of New Place, Shakespeare's retirement home, where he died in 1616. This site is slightly confusing, as the house no longer exists. The remaining property is Nash House, home of Thomas Nash, husband of Shakespeare's granddaughter, Elizabeth Hall. New Place was demolished in the 18th century when the owner became fed up with tourists gawping over his wall. Only the gardens remain and provide a peaceful haven of escape from the crowds.

4. Continue along Chapel Street and pause for a moment by the junction of Sheep Street and High Street. Ely Street was previously known as Swine Street, and housed the pig market. Sheep Street played host to a sheep market originating around 1265. Harvard House, next door to the Garrick Inn, was built in 1596 by Thomas Rogers, a prosperous merchant in Shakespeare's time, and is a splendid example of a late Elizabethan town house. It is also the birthplace of Katherine Rogers, the mother of John Harvard who founded the American University of the same name. The Midland Bank is surmounted by an interesting carved frieze of scenes from Shakespeare's plays. Turn left up Ely Street and at a T-junction, turn right along Rother Street past the Civic Hall to reach the ornate American Fountain by the market place.

Modern traders set up stalls here every Friday but it used to be a cattle market. Rother is the old English word for cattle but any resemblance to the tourists tramping through is purely coincidental.

5. Cross Wood Street, pass left of the Nat West Bank and go down The Minories, an alleyway which leads to Henley Street, emerging by Shakespeare's Birthplace. Surrounded by gift shops, this isolated timber building struggles to recreate the atmosphere of the period. You won't find the spirit of Shakespeare among the crowds traipsing through the Birthplace, but you may experience it on a quiet evening in Holy Trinity churchyard overlooking the river. Or during one of his plays, performed so powerfully by the RSC. Turn right along Henley Street past the library to reach the roundabout by Barclays Bank. The house on the opposite corner belonged to Judith Quiney, Shakespeare's daughter, who married a vintner, Thomas Quiney. It is now, surprise, surprise, a gift shop. Cross Union Street and continue ahead down Bridge Street, which was part of the old Roman road leading to the original ford over the river. At one time, Bridge Street was divided into two roads, known as Fore and Back Bridge Street, with a line of shops down the middle but these were demolished in the 19th century. This explains the unusual width of the current thoroughfare. At the far end of Bridge Street is the TIC and the start.

Tanworth in Arden

Access

Tanworth in Arden (SP 114705 – OS Landranger 139) is located off the A435 and B4101, 4 miles north-east of Redditch. Limited parking is possible around the village green. Buses run to Redditch. The village lies between Danzey Green and Wood End railway stations.

The Village

Tanworth in Arden is tucked away in an unspoilt corner of Warwickshire. A perfect blend of black and white timber framed houses and Georgian buildings of varying ages and styles nestle amid tree lined roads. Originally a clearing in the Forest of Arden, the village stands on high open ground and marvellous views can be enjoyed from the churchyard. The young chestnut tree on the charming village green replaces an earlier specimen, planted to commemorate Victoria's Jubilee.

Several buildings have names which give a clue as to their former use, Doctor's House, The Old Boot Shop, The School House, The Old Work House and The Old Bakehouse. The "in-Arden" was added in the 19th century to avoid confusion with Tamworth in neighbouring Staffordshire.

Nearby Attractions

Earlswood Lakes (SP 115738), a few miles north, are home to many wildfowl and this is a particularly good location for seeing resident great crested grebes. In spring, you may be rewarded with the enchanting sight of the fluffy youngsters being carried, piggy-back style, on the adult's back. The paths around the lakes can be muddy; wellies are essential in winter.

Warning to fast walkers!

Clowes Wood (SP 102745), criss-crossed by paths, is a marvellous mixed woodland owned by the Warwickshire Wildlife Trust. A walk through the oak, birch, beech and alder trees is particularly rewarding with plenty to interest both the birdwatcher and botanist. Both these attractions can be easily reached from The Lakes and Earlswood railway stations.

The Trail

1. The Trail starts by the village green. The walk uses a couple of stiles but an alternative (marked on the map) is to nip down Doctor's Hill, joining the rest of the Trail by the farm. For the full circuit, walk past the village stores and war memorial. By the green, The Bell has an excellent varied menu, but you haven't earned any imbibing yet, so onward! Follow the road as it bends right. Ignore the left turn, Bates Lane, and continue down Vicarage Hill. Walk past Whalebone Cottage with its fantastic garden entrance.

2. Just past the Old Vicarage, on the left, go over a stile on the right

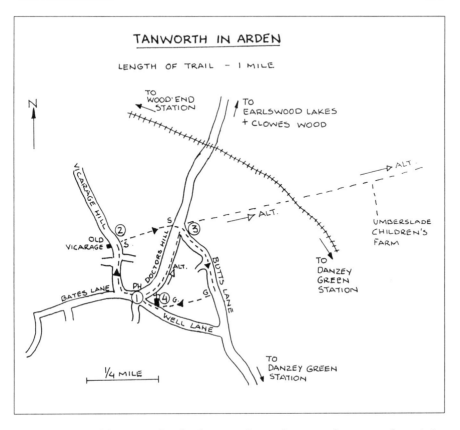

TANWORTH IN ARDEN

LENGTH OF TRAIL - I MILE

into a field. Keep the hedge on the right, past houses, then join another hedge line going left downhill. At the bottom of the field, go over a stile in the right corner, (ignore a stile away to the left). Emerge onto the road. Umberslade Children's Farm opposite is well worth a visit but make sure you don't break the public footpath speed limit as you walk down the drive! The farm, open daily from March to September and at weekends in October, is an excellent place for children to learn about livestock and the changes that have affected agriculture in the last 50 years. There's also a coffee shop. The magnificent poplar trees you pass once lined the drive to Umberslade Hall. The home of the Archer family for over six centuries, the Hall is now converted into luxury apartments. (A pleasant walk continues up the drive, past an old gateway to the Hall and returns across fields).

3. To continue the Trail, return to the road junction and go left down
    Butts Lane, signed to Danzey Green. Walk past the school and
    continue down the narrow lane. Go through a kissing gate on the
    right, half hidden behind a marker post, and head past a lone tree
    and up the field with a fence on the right. As you reach a gate
    into the churchyard, glance behind to savour the extensive views.

4. No less an authority than Pevsner was puzzled by the architecture
    of this 14th century limestone church of St Mary Magdalene. The
    spire was rebuilt in 1720 and is a notable landmark for miles
    around. In the spacious interior is an impressive, if rather grue-
    some, monument to the Archer family. The chief glory is the
    glowing, stained glass; take time to absorb the detail and you'll
    notice the remarkable three-dimensional effect. Either side of the
    high altar are two unusual pedestals, which still show traces of
    the original mediaeval colouring. These probably once bore stat-
    ues. A previous incumbent in the 1780s was the Reverend Phillip
    Wren, a great grandson of the architect. The village green, the
    start of the Trail and that promised refreshment is beyond the
    church.

Tredington

Access

Tredington (SP 258436 – OS Landranger 151) lies just off the busy A3400, 3 miles north of Shipston on Stour. Buses to Shipston, Oxford and Stratford call here. Very limited parking is possible by the church.

The Village

Tredington, nestling in the valley of the river Stour, is one of the most picturesque villages in the county. It has a long and interesting history dating back to Saxon times. For almost a thousand years, the parish was owned by successive Bishops of Worcester, including Wulstan. The Fosse Way passes close by and the river Stour forms the eastern boundary. Situated close to Shipston, Tredington was on the line of the Birmingham to Oxford and London mail coach runs. This turnpike road is now the busy A3400 which slices the village in two, creating two distinct halves. The newer houses lie to the west and the older, prettier corner occupies a maze of narrow lanes to the east. The setting around the village green and church exudes a timeless charm and has become an irresistible subject for many calendars. The thatched cottages and colourful gardens draw many visitors. Comprehensive booklets on the history of the church and village are on sale in the church. Old photographs in the guide show how little has changed, although the main road does look slightly different!

By the 11th century, three mills were in operation in Tredington. The remaining mill building was converted into dwellings after the last miller, William Hodges, died in 1940. Along with much of rural England, Tredington suffered considerably at the time of the Black Death. The old parish was once isolated in the county of Gloucestershire until Tredington was absorbed into Warwickshire in 1931.

Cottages in Tredington

Along with other Warwickshire villages, Tredington boasts a wealth of folklore. In the early part of this century, a villager, Betty Lofs, was suspected of being a witch. Disliked by the other inhabitants, Betty wasn't invited to a party but came anyway in the form of a cat, which was later wounded in the paw by a man with a pitchfork. The cat disappeared but Betty was seen the next day with a bandaged hand – allegedly!

Nearby Attractions

Idlicote (SP 285444) is a pleasant hamlet to the east of Tredington. Walks from here across rolling countryside are particularly enjoyable.

A visit to the nearby village of Whatcote (SP 300446) is also recommended. This peaceful spot seems an unlikely target for the might of the German airforce but during the Second World War the church was unlucky enough to suffer a direct hit from a bomb.

The Trail

1. The Trail starts from the church of St Gregory's. Of astonishing size and seemingly out of all proportion to this small village, it reflects the fact that the parish of Tredington once included many surrounding hamlets. There has been a place of worship on this site since Saxon times and restorations at the end of the last century revealed some intriguing features. Important rare remains of Anglo-Danish windows and two doors would be remarkable enough but they are also 20 feet above ground, over the nave arcades. This suggests that access was possible only through these upper doors, presumably to prevent attacks by marauding Danes. The interior is spacious and light with magnificent Norman piers. The Norman south doorway is enriched by zigzag carvings, unusually added by the Victorians; normally Victorian restorers could ruin the character of any building. The elaborately carved canopied pulpit dates from the 17th century. The octagonal font is a remarkable structure and the brasses are also impressive. The spire is the church's crowning glory, soaring to a height of 210 feet, making it a distinctive landmark visible throughout the surrounding countryside. Tredington parish was once the richest living in the district, and at one time supported two rectors, which didn't lead to a very harmonious situation. At one stage, both rectors tried to preach simultaneously, one at either end of the church, which must have made for a lively Sunday service. Presumably if the parishioners became bored, they could wander from one to the other – a kind of embryonic Hyde Park Speakers' Corner!

2. With your back to the church, turn right and follow the road as it bears left in front of Manor Farm, one of the oldest buildings in the village. Continue down the narrow lane passing pretty thatched cottages.

3. On reaching a small green, bear right along a street lined with grass verges, past Orchard Croft. You also walk by Green Cottages and The Old House, another early dwelling, once occupied by Mr Ravenscroft, a miller from Birmingham. Head up the main road, emerging by the post office. Turn left past the White Lion Inn and the thatched cottages straddling this busy road.

4. At the next junction, turn left down a delightful lane to the church and the start. On the way, pass the Old School House, still with a bell on the gable end. Before leaving the village, it's worth walking down Mill Close to the right of the church for a different view of the church. But you'll need a wide angle lens to fit this towering spire into any photograph.

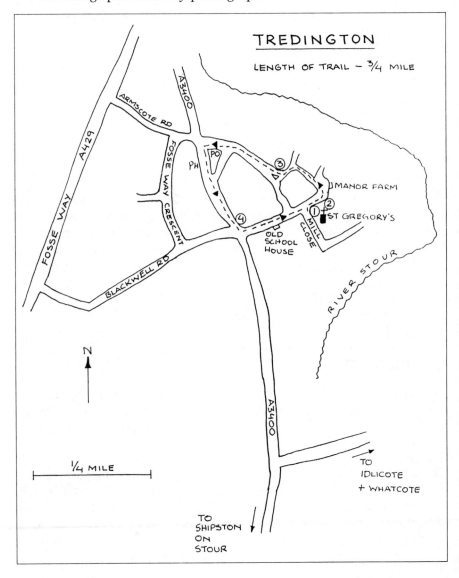

The Tysoes

Access

Middle and Upper Tysoe (SP 339442 – OS Landranger 151) lie amid a tangle of minor roads, south of the A422, 10 miles east of Shipston on Stour. Limited bus service to Shipston and Stratford. Street parking is possible near the pub.

The Village

As with Brailes, there are in fact three Tysoes; Middle, Lower and Upper. Tysoe means Tiw's spur of land. Tiw was a Saxon god of war whose name still exists in the word Tuesday. The Tysoes are clustered at the foot of the Edge Hill escarpment in one of the most

St Mary's church, Middle Tysoe

attractive areas of Warwickshire, which is known as the Vale of the Red Horse after the figure of a horse was cut into the soil on Sunrising Hill. The figure disappeared under the plough around 1800 before it had the chance to become a tourist attraction like the one at Westbury. At around 100 yards long and 70 yards high, the horse must have been an impressive sight.

Nearby Lower Tysoe was previously known as Temple Tysoe because it was owned by the Knights Templar order of Crusader Knights. In mediaeval times, the Tysoes ranked in importance alongside Brailes as a settlement. Our Trail tours Middle and Upper Tysoe, twin villages now expanded into virtually one community.

Nearby Attractions

An attractive walk across fields leads from Middle Tysoe to the windmill on Windmill Hill (SP 332428). From here you are treated to stunning views of Compton Wynyates, surely a Hollywood producer's dream of an English mansion! Many writers have described this house as the most beautiful they've ever seen, and it's hard to disagree. The setting is perfect, the house nestling in a bowl in the hills, but it's no longer open to the public. Another walk from Upper Tysoe leads to Compton Wynyates church.

A country house you *can* visit is Upton House (SP 370457), a National Trust property containing magnificent collections of porcelain and paintings. The beautiful gardens, full of mature trees and splendid floral displays, are well worth exploring. Open from April to October, from Saturday to Wednesday.

The Trail

1.   The Trail starts outside the Peacock Inn, a lively pub which serves both communities. The wall sign of The Peacock Inn is striking and much larger than most signs. With the pub to the left, walk up the main street past Meg Rivers Cakes and the Health Centre to reach the graceful church of St Mary's. Built of local Hornton stone, this contains brasses, corbels and an 18th century bellcote. Notice the restored pinnacles and parapets outside and the unusual interior, scraped back to the masonry beneath. The elaborate octagonal font is decorated with carved figures and

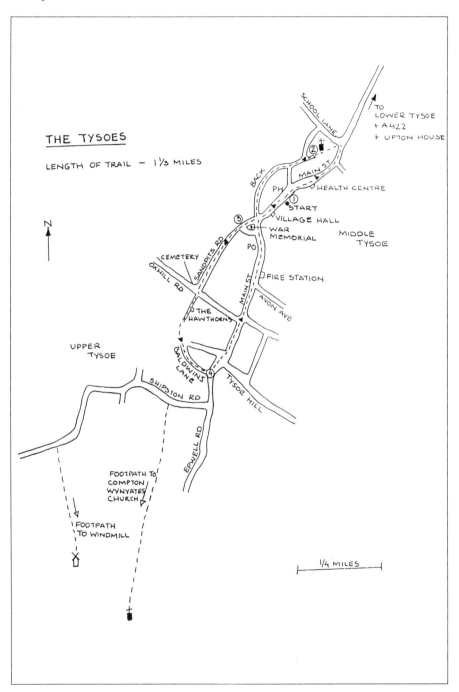

THE TYSOES

LENGTH OF TRAIL — 1⅓ MILES

surmounted by a tall, ornately pinnacled cover. The churchyard is particularly beautiful, awash with primroses in spring. A Saxon preaching cross in the churchyard shelters under the yew tree and there are mediaeval tombstones to puzzle over. St Mary's is one of many churches in Warwickshire which hosts summer concerts.

2. With your back to the church door, turn right and go through the iron gate into a quiet lane. Further down the lane on the right, on the apex of a thatched roof is the figure of a peacock, the thatcher's signature. Where the lane bends left, keep ahead down an alley-way leading to a charming thatched cottage. Turn left down Back Lane to reach the war memorial in front of picturesque thatched cottages, one of which has another "signature", a fox running across the roof. These figures add a quirky touch to the village architecture.

3. Turn right up Sandpits Road, signed to Oxhill, soon passing two old drinking troughs, a his and hers perhaps? This peaceful residential street leads to a junction by a cemetery. Cross over and go down an alleyway left of telephone poles and alongside the drive to The Hawthorns. The alleyway zigzags to reach a gravel drive. Bear left to join a tarmac lane. Walk ahead (not left) along Baldwins Lane to emerge into Upper Tysoe. (If you turn right and follow the road right you will reach a wooden signpost marking the start of the footpath to Compton Wynyates church).

4. To continue the Trail, turn left and continue along the main road into Middle Tysoe passing a playing field, tennis courts and a fire station. Along with the station at Fenny Compton, this is also struggling to survive in the face of local government cuts. Go past a post office and shop to the earlier junction by the war memorial. Keep on the main village street past an old fountain, festooned with religious quotations, to pass the village hall. On the left is a small Reading Room bought as a tangible memorial to the villagers who gave their lives in World War 1. Their names are recorded on a plaque outside. Continue past the pub to reach the start.

Warmington

Access

Warmington (SP 411477 – OS Landranger 151) is located just off the B4100, 5 miles north of Banbury. Considerate parking is possible in the main street near the pub. Limited bus service to Banbury and Southam.

The Village

The ancient monastic settlement of Warmington, hidden away amid fertile farmland at the foot of Edge Hill, is one of the loveliest in Warwickshire. The scene around the green, the honey-coloured houses and the duck pond reflect a subtle, untouched beauty which

Cottages around the village green

adds to the timeless atmosphere. The ducks, which make the pond their home, have an uncanny instinct about the contents of rucksacks and mug anyone who ventures near.

Warmington has a lengthy history and was found worthy of a mention in the Domesday Book. The lord of the manor, the Earl of Warwick, gave the lands to St Peter's Abbey in Preaux, Normandy, which his father had endowed. Foundations of a small priory were discovered in Court Close when new houses were built in the 1950s. The monks also built the church while the manor remained in monastic hands for around 450 years.

Nearby Attractions

To the south-west can be found the neat Oxfordshire village of Hornton (SP 394450), with a trim green, thatched cottages and a 17th Century manor house, all built out of the distinctive ochre coloured Hornton stone. The 12th century church contains a mediaeval Doom painting which is still in remarkable condition.

Farnborough Hall (SP 430495), home of the Holbech family since 1684, is a National Trust property. The chief glory is the landscaped gardens and terrace walk decorated with ornamental temples and offering glorious views. Open from April to the end of September, on Wednesdays and Saturdays while the Terrace Walk only may be visited on Thursday and Friday during this period.

The Trail

1. The Trail starts outside The Plough. Along with Ratley, this is another pub haunted by the ghost of a Civil War soldier. With the pub to the left, walk down the hill to the delightful green, complete with duckpond, old sheep dip and commemorative signpost for a past Best Kept Village competition. Scattered about the village are several plaques and trees planted in recognition of previous awards, a testament to the pride which the local community feels for its village.

2. At the end of the green, bear left down the lane signed to Banbury. The constant background roar on this section is a sign of "progress", a tangible reminder of the M40 slicing through the valley

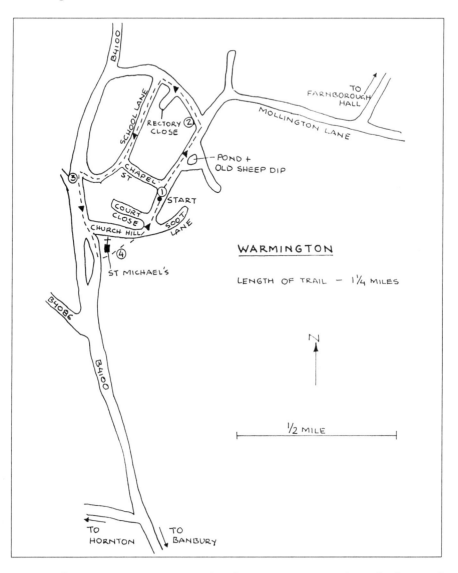

to the east. Its presence is hard to ignore, even though the road isn't visible from the village. Go past Rectory Close and turn left at the next junction into School Lane. This leads uphill past charming cottages with the church dominating the view ahead. Continue up the hill past Springfield House with an old drinking trough opposite. The road bends right to join the B4100.

3. Turn left along the pavement; a mercifully brief section as the road is noisy and the traffic, as usual, travels too fast. At the next corner, take the steps ahead, or the gentle slope on the right, into the churchyard. St Michael's Church stands sentinel above the village, although it's not clear why the church was built so far away from the heart of the village. Inside can be seen interesting carvings on the piscina and sedilia stone seats. The wooden screen under the chancel arch is all that remains of a massive rood-screen, destroyed following the Reformation. To the right of the chancel arch is the chopped off doorway and stairway which once led to the loft over the rood-screen. In the steep, sloping churchyard the line of pine trees marks the limit of the original churchyard. Many of the gravestones nearest the church go back several centuries, and a few are still legible, one to the Thomas family dating to 1633. It is believed a mass grave contains some of the fallen soldiers from Edgehill. There is also a memorial to Captain Gourdin who died of his wounds in the same battle.

4. At the rear of the churchyard, follow a steep path down steps, which can be slippery in wet weather. Emerge onto a lane. Ignore Soot Lane on the right, and go down the hill passing the Village Hall and pub to reach the start.

Warwick

Access

Warwick (SP 287648 – OS Landranger 151), best reached off the A46, lies 2 miles west of Leamington Spa. Pay and display parking is well signed. Warwick is served by an excellent bus service connecting to much of Warwickshire. National Express coaches also call and there is a railway station, making it a marvellous centre for a holiday.

The Town

Steeped in history, the county town of Warwick is full of beautiful and interesting buildings. The town grew up around the site of the castle which developed near the river in 1068. Today, Warwick Castle is one of the most popular attractions in the Midlands and the town inevitably suffers from its own popularity during the summer. A visit to the castle is a must, regardless of this Trail, but you'll appreciate the sense of history more if you can visit during a quieter time.

The Town suffered its own Great Fire of 1694 and was almost completely rebuilt, although past writers have claimed this proved quite beneficial because it removed many of the timber houses cluttered at the centre, and allowed fine brick and stone houses to take their place. The grand St Mary's Church occupies the prime position and it is this rather than the castle which dominates all approach roads to the town. At least a full day is needed to see everything of interest, although even after countless visits I still discover something new each time.

Nearby Attractions

Hatton Locks (SP 244669) on the Grand Union Canal can be reached

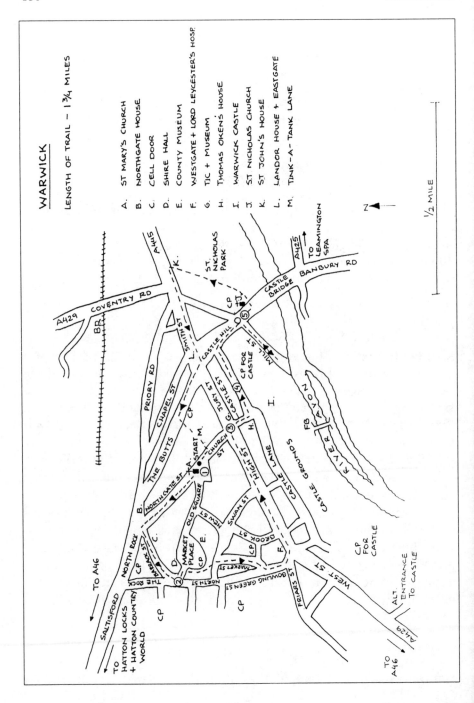

WARWICK

LENGTH OF TRAIL — 1¾ MILES

A. ST MARY'S CHURCH
B. NORTHGATE HOUSE
C. CELL DOOR
D. SHIRE HALL
E. COUNTY MUSEUM
F. WESTGATE + LORD LEYCESTER'S HOSP.
G. TIC + MUSEUM
H. THOMAS OKEN'S HOUSE
I. WARWICK CASTLE
J. ST NICHOLAS CHURCH
K. ST JOHN'S HOUSE
L. LANDOR HOUSE + EASTGATE
M. TINK-A-TANK LANE

½ MILE

via a charming towpath walk. The Locks, traditionally known as the Stairway to Heaven, must be a daunting sight for approaching boats. After negotiating the 21 locks which ascend 146 feet over 2 miles, visitors may choose a different nickname.

Hatton Country World (SP 235664), near Hatton Locks, is well worth a visit. Open most days, there is a craft centre, pets' corner, adventure playground, cafe and nature trail.

The Trail

1. The Trail starts from St Mary's Church which amply justifies its reputation as the most magnificent church in the county. The breathtaking Beauchamp chapel should on no account be missed. Alabaster tombs of quite magnificent workmanship commemorate Thomas Beauchamp, a Commander at the Battle of Crecy in 1346, and his wife Katherine. The chapel also contains an ornate effigy of Richard, Earl of Warwick. The Regimental Chapel of the Royal Warwickshire Regiment displays the garter banner of Field Marshal Montgomery. The minute Dean's chapel is a remarkable example of painstaking craftsmanship. If you have a head for heights and enough puff, climb the 160 steps of the tower which soars majestically over the surrounding countryside. Open occasionally during the year, visitors can appreciate fantastic views including a different perspective of the castle. Turn right from the church down Northgate Street, which is fronted by fine Georgian houses. At the end, Northgate House has an unusual painted sundial set in an oval cartouche. Turn left into Barrack Street, where the original cell door from the jail can be seen. This was also the site of the gallows at a time when public executions were a popular source of entertainment, before the advent of television.

2. Turn left under the archway of the Shire Hall. The elegant house of Abbotsford was built in 1714 but the hideous bridge connecting it to the Shire Hall is obviously modern. Across the Market Place is the County Museum which houses a model of Warwick as it looked before the great fire, so you can make up your own mind which version you prefer. It also contains displays on local history and archaeology, as well as the Sheldon tapestry map of

Lord Leycester's Hospital

Warwickshire, completed in 1588. Go down Market Street and turn left to reach Westgate, which along with Eastgate are the only town gates to survive. The Victorian pillarboxes here and in Eastgate retain the original vertical slots. Turn left past Westgate to Lord Leycester's Hospital which, in 1571, was owned by Robert Dudley, Earl of Leicester, and converted into almshouses for old soldiers. They continue to serve that purpose today. Among the beautiful timbers of the hospital is a rather odd feature; a garish blue porcupine. This strange creature is the family crest of the Sidneys, whose family remain patrons to this day. You can also visit the 14th century chapel above Westgate through the Hospital. Among many features of note are carved bench ends of a seated bear and ragged staff; the family crest of the Dudleys. Walk up the High Street to the junction with Castle Street.

3.   On the corner, in the Court House are the Town and Yeomanry Museums, plus the Tourist Information Centre. The Court House was built in the early 1700s by Francis Smith, a well known architect responsible for many fine buildings in Warwick and elsewhere in the Midlands. Ahead, Jury Street (once known as

Jewry Street) was where the Jewish population was concentrated. Turn right down Castle Street to pass Thomas Oken's house, at the corner of Castle Street and Castle Lane. This mid 16th century timber framed house was the home of one of Warwick's main benefactors and now houses The Doll Museum, which is open all year. Turn left along Castle Lane, passing one of the entrances to Warwick Castle.

4. Warwick Castle is a magnificent edifice with a long and venerable history. The original construction was fortified by Ethelfleda, daughter of King Alfred in 914 and in the 13th century it was attacked during the Barons' war with Henry III. The mighty Beauchamp family reinforced and extended the castle. When the Earl of Warwick (the Kingmaker) died, the castle passed through many hands including Ambrose Dudley and Sir Fulke Greville. In 1642, the Royalists laid siege to the castle and in 1978 it was sold to Madame Tussaud's. The Kingmaker exhibition is particularly suitable for children and brings the sights, and smells, of history to life. The parkland was landscaped by Capability Brown and the 60 acres offer an escape from the bustle of the interior. The entrance fee may seem expensive but you do get a lot for your money. At the end of Castle Lane, turn right down Castle Hill to the bridge to enjoy one of the finest views of the castle, one that appears on all the postcards. Also worth a look is Mill Street with its timber framed houses, some predating the Great Fire. Some of the gardens are occasionally open to the public in aid of charity.

5. Cross by the roundabout and turn right past St Nicholas Church and left into the car park by St Nicholas Park. Follow the signs through the car park to St John's House museum of costume and folk life, where admission is free. This building was the site of a hospital founded in 1175, which gave lodging and refreshment to poor travellers. Turn left down Smith Street passing Landor House, the birthplace in 1775 of the poet, Walter Savage Landor. Walk past Eastgate. Turn right down The Butts and halfway along, look for an alleyway on the left, Tink-a-tank Lane. Clatter down here in clogs, if anyone still wears them these days, and you'll realise how this narrow passageway got its onomatopoeic name. This leads to the churchyard of St Mary's and the start.

Welford on Avon

Access

Welford on Avon (SP 145522 – OS Landranger 151) lies 4 miles west of Stratford upon Avon, just off the B439 and is on a bus route between Stratford and Evesham. Considerate parking is possible near the maypole or along Headland Road.

The Village

The beautiful village of Welford on Avon is part of the rich market garden area of the Avon valley. Set on the banks of the river, its charming thatched cottages are extremely photogenic and have appeared on numerous calendars.

The lands were given in 1059 to the Saxon priory of Deerhurst, near Tewkesbury, by the Earl of Gloucester, since when it has passed through many hands.

Nearby Attractions

Binton (SP145540), 2 miles north, is worth a visit to see the memorial window in St Peter's Church which commemorates one of this century's most profound tragedies. This window to Captain Robert Falcon Scott, whose wife Kathleen was the rector's sister, was unveiled in 1915 and tells the story of his ill fated attempt to reach the south pole.

A delightful riverside path heads west from Welford, eventually reaching Barton and Bidford on Avon (featured in an earlier chapter). An enjoyable full day could be spent visiting Welford, then following the river to Bidford. Both villages have plenty of places to eat and are an excellent introduction to this wonderful valley.

The Trail

1. The Trail starts from the prominent 65 feet maypole near the Shakespeare Inn. The maypole is said to have existed in the 14th century and is still in use today, although it sways alarmingly in high winds. Stand with the Maypole Stores on the left and turn right along the High Street passing the Memorial Hall. The plaques on the wall commemorate Welford's win in a previous Best Kept Village award.

2. Turn left before the post office and Bell Inn into Church Street, passing delightful black and white half timbered cottages. At the end of Church Street, walk past St Peter's. All that remains of the original Saxon church, built by the Priory of Deerhurst, is the font bowl. The later Norman replacement, built in the 12th century, was altered considerably in the 1860s and suffered a disastrous fire in the tower in 1884. Except for its vivid stained glass windows, the interior is otherwise unremarkable. The colourful east window dates from 1924 and is by the artist, Geoffrey Webb while another window commemorates the distinguished polar

St Peter's church

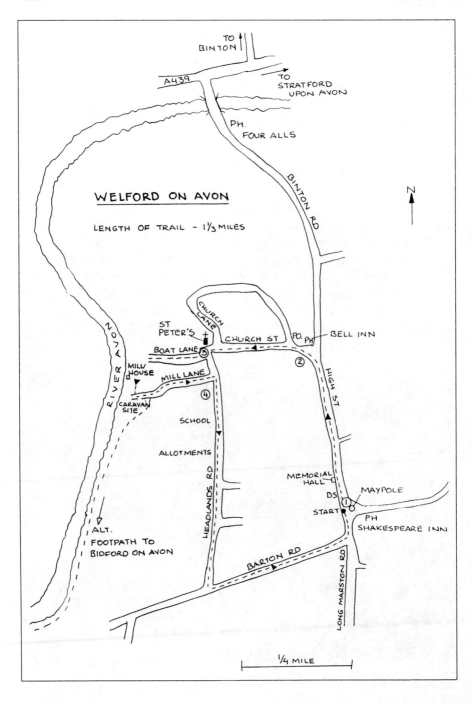

explorer Wally Herbert. In complete contrast, the south aisle window depicts carved heads of Henry VI and his French Queen, Margaret of Anjou, hauntingly described by Shakespeare as the "she-wolf of France" with a "tiger's heart wrapped in a woman's hide". The splendid 14th century lychgate eventually became unsafe and the gate you see today is an exact replica, built by local craftsmen. On the wall by the gate, a blue plaque marks the site of the old village pound and stocks.

3. Continue past the church and walk ahead into Boat Lane, where the half timbered cottages and colourful gardens may seem vaguely familiar. This picturesque, relatively unspoilt scene has appeared on the usual array of postcards, calendars and chocolate boxes. At the end of Boat Lane, turn left along a gravel path by a garden and enjoy your first view over the river. Walk past Mill House and on reaching Mill Lane, turn left past the entrance to a caravan site. (The walk along the river to Bidford begins through the caravan park). At the end of Mill Lane, turn right into Headland Road (where there is alternative parking).

4. Walk past a school and allotments and turn left at the T-junction along Barton Road, and left again into the High Street to the start. Alternative refreshment is available at the Four Alls which is not on the Trail but easily reached by the river bridge, just off the B439. It's worth visiting for its stained glass window (yes, this is a pub, not a church). In the bar are four stained glass portraits of a soldier, parson, king and countryman, with the appropriate legend "Fight All, Pray All, Rule All, Pay All" hence the name of the pub, the Four Alls.

Wellesbourne

Access

Wellesbourne (SP 280555 – OS Landranger 151) is 6 miles east of Stratford upon Avon at the junction of the B4086 and B4087, now bypassed by the A429. A good selection of buses run to Stratford, Warwick, Leamington, Kenilworth, Coventry and Kineton. Street parking is possible near the church on Church Street.

The Village

Wellesbourne is a large, straggling village which conceals its treasures from passing motorists, who remain blissfully unaware of the fascinating corners to be explored. Once two smaller villages, Wellesbourne Hastings and Wellesbourne Mountford, which grew up around a crossing over the river Dene and the charming Chestnut Square. In the last 30 years the two villages have grown considerably and are now known simply as Wellesbourne. Excellent guides, available in the village, detail the history of both Wellesbournes, and will add immeasurably to your appreciation of this intriguing community.

Nearby Attractions

Charlecote Park (SP 260564), a few miles north, is a National Trust property open from April to the end of October, between Friday and Tuesday. The current house was built by Sir Thomas Lucy in 1558 but the Lucy family have owned the manor since the 13th century. The adjoining deer park attracts many visitors.

The restored Wellesbourne Watermill (SP 284545), a couple of miles south off the B4086, is well worth a visit. As well as demonstrations of traditional crafts such as chair bodging and hurdle making, there are gardens, falconry demonstrations and an owl

Chestnut Square

sanctuary to enjoy. A tea shop provides refreshments. Open from April to the end of September, with limited access during the winter.

The nearby Wellesbourne airfield has a museum open on Sundays and Bank Holidays.

The Trail

1. The Trail starts outside the church in Church Street. This area around the church was part of the old village of Wellesbourne Hastings. Enter the churchyard, passing on the right an overgrown table tomb decorated with a skull and bones. The church porch is protected by unusual iron gates painted blue which are sadly often padlocked. Dating from the 12th century, St Peter's was almost entirely rebuilt in the 1840s. Graced with a spacious interior and a beautiful Norman chancel arch, another feature of note is the sanctuary with a marble arcade inlaid with a gold mosaic. The stained glass windows are also of interest. Continue past the door and war memorial to a gate in the top left corner of the churchyard.

2. Walk up the fenced path to cross the footbridge. Brawles Meadow
    exudes an air of tranquillity which seems a million miles away
    from Wellesbourne's bustling centre. Turn left alongside the
    brook on a path which leads to a gravelled lane. Keep ahead onto
    Church Walk where those who have dismissed Wellesbourne as
    modern and uninteresting will be pleasantly surprised. These

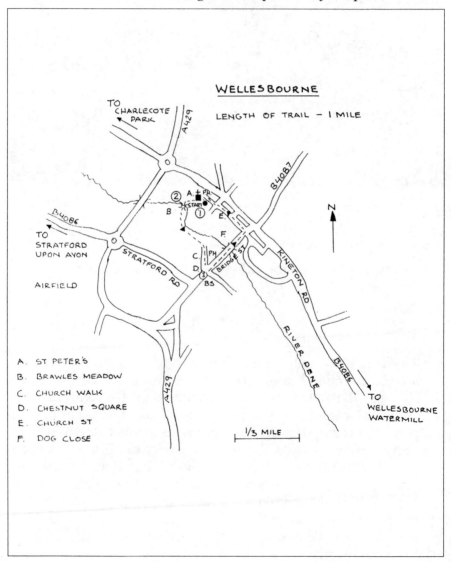

A. ST PETER'S
B. BRAWLES MEADOW
C. CHURCH WALK
D. CHESTNUT SQUARE
E. CHURCH ST
F. DOG CLOSE

cottages have changed little and are a delightful mix of thatched, half timbered and brick which makes as pleasing a picture as you will find anywhere. Buckle House may have been refronted with brick in the 18th century, but the core of the building dates back even earlier.

3. This lane leads to Chestnut Square, where the Stag's Head pub is a pleasant spot to sit and study the fascinating architecture around the Square. Pitt House is of particular interest. Once the home of the Reverend John Clavering, curate of nearby Moreton Morrell, the name of the house comes from a later owner, Richard Pitt, a doctor. The Red House next door was once the home of Thomas Ayleworth, the last in a long line of Ayleworths, an important local family. The Square was the setting for the first meeting in 1872 of the agricultural workers' trade union, set up by Joseph Arch. A commemorative tablet has been placed rather incongruously in the bus shelter. The chestnut tree is a replacement for the original which died in 1949. To continue, turn left up Bridge Street past the Manor House, occupied by the Venour family who also owned considerable land in the area. After the family line died out, it was bought by the Reverend John Lucy who demolished the original building. Walk over the road bridge, back across Wellesbourne Brook; this is the spot which links the two Wellesbournes. Go past the shop and Methodist church to reach the one-way system.

4. Cross Bridge Street with care and turn left down Church Street, passing interesting old cottages on the left. Behind these cottages is Dog Close, a valuable open space at the heart of the village. Where the road swings right, keep left down Church Street past the White House and White Cottage to reach the start by the church. The King's Head pub at the end of this lane unusually backs onto the churchyard entrance, although I'm sure the congregation appreciates this proximity.

Wootton Wawen

Access

Wootton Wawen (SP 150632 – OS Landranger 151) is on the A3400, 6 miles north of Stratford upon Avon. Limited parking is available outside the church, but please be considerate if a service is in progress. Good bus service between Stratford and Birmingham. The railway line between Stratford and Birmingham runs through but the station, half a mile to the west of the village, is a request stop.

The Village

Although last in the book, Wootton Wawen is by no means least. Beautiful and full of character, this is also one of the oldest settlements in Warwickshire, with a long history as an agricultural community. The nearby country estates employed much of the village workforce and the osier beds on the river provided the basis for a thriving hurdle-making industry. Today, the village still prospers, housing several cottage industries and catering for the needs of many canal boats. In the past, the River Alne would have been larger and until the first bridge was built, the river flooded regularly. Even today, the minor roads near the river can be closed following heavy rain.

In Church Field were the remains of a mediaeval priory, established by a Benedictine Abbey based in Normandy. By 1840, little remained except traces of a pool, which was in turn obliterated by roadworks in the 1960s. Excavations have also revealed the possible site of a Saxon monastic complex. The Stratford Canal passes through the village via an aqueduct, built in 1813, high above the busy A3400 road. Wootton Wawen suffers from a great deal of traffic. A brief halt alongside the bridge will convince anyone that there should be a 30mph speed limit through this, and any village.

Nearby Attractions

This stretch of the Stratford upon Avon Canal is lovely and a walk in either direction along its towpath is especially rewarding.

Aston Cantlow village (SP 138599), to the south-west, is a charming community reached by riverside paths from Wootton Wawen. It is generally believed that John Shakespeare, William's father, and Mary Arden were married in the church.

The Trail

1. The Trail, which takes the form of a figure of eight, starts from the church. If arriving by train, join the Trail by the Bull's Head pub (see the map). The site of St Peter's was first used by monks who were given the land by Aethelbald, King of Mercia, in the early 8th century. Its Saxon origins can be seen in the base of the tower. The interior is every bit as rewarding as the exterior, with a conglomeration of almost every style of architecture. The numerous monuments include an alabaster 15th century knight and 16th century brasses of the Harewell family. Adorning each side of the west window are carved stone heads said to be those of Edward III and his Queen, Philippa. Behind the church is a fascinating old timber framed porch. In the churchyard lies the grave of Henry Houghton who was injured at Waterloo (presumably the battle, not the station, although he could have been an early victim of London's rush hour). Walk through the well tended churchyard and follow a path which bends left by the caravan park, down a tarmac lane to the main road.

2. Cross over and turn left past The Glebe to reach the Bull's Head on the corner. A very attractive building, this is one of the oldest pubs in Warwickshire, dating back to 1387. It is also extremely popular, offering an excellent choice of food. (The lane from the station emerges by the pub). Bear left with the main road, passing a house with a huge sundial under the gable, which helpfully gives the house its name. Walk past the village shop. The scene on the left, with the war memorial, the Lodge building and church presents an ageless charm. Continue past the bus stop and cross over, turning right alongside the wall surrounding Wootton Hall.

Wootton Hall Lodge

Now almost obscured by caravans, the Hall, built in Italianate style in 1637, comes complete with ornamental weir and lake. This is fed by the river Alne and known as the Serpentine, although it's slightly smaller than its celebrated namesake in Hyde Park. Mrs Fitzherbert spent her childhood at the Hall. She is better known as the wife of the Prince of Wales, (later George IV). Their secret marriage in 1785 lasted until 1803. The story goes that she may be the ghost of a grey lady who haunts the Hall.

3. Continue over the bridge and spend a few minutes drinking in the lovely waterfalls. Keen eyes may spot herons, moorhens and both pied and grey wagtails searching for insects along the water's edge. The next few buildings passed, on both sides of the road, are old mill houses which make distinctive private dwellings, one of which boasts an elaborate shield on the wall. You will soon pass a small chapel and shop to reach a minor crossroads. The impressive aqueduct ahead conveys the Stratford Canal over the main road. Those of a nervous disposition may find themselves checking the state of the brickwork supports as the traffic thunders past. Just beyond the bridge is The Navigation Inn, another

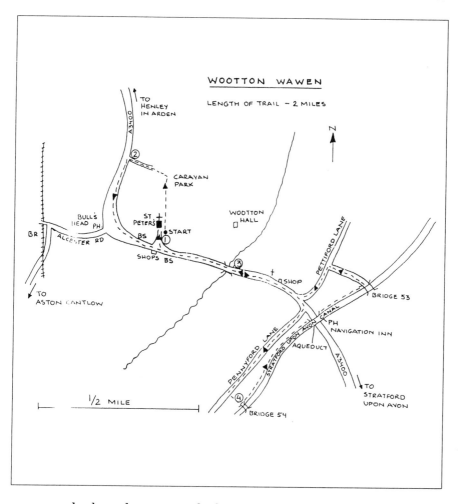

popular hostelry next to the busy canal marina. Turn right down the blessedly quiet Pennyford Lane for about a quarter of a mile. Just past a few houses on the left, turn left down a lane to reach a canal bridge (number 54).

4. Turn left down the towpath, passing across the aqueduct for a bird's eye view of the road. Continue to the next split bridge, (number 53) and turn left down the lane to emerge at the other end of Pettiford Lane. Turn left and shortly emerge by the earlier junction where a right turn leads back to the start.

More Discovery Trails

TOWN & VILLAGE DISCOVERY TRAILS are for walkers with shoes, rather than boots. They visit some of the most attractive towns and villages of England, enabling the visitor on foot to discover what car drivers and fast-paced ramblers often miss. Titles in this series are all £6.95 and currently include:

TOWN & VILLAGE DISCOVERY TRAILS: Cumbria & the Lake District
Norman Buckley

TOWN & VILLAGE DISCOVERY TRAILS: The Peak District
Norman James & Abigail Bristow

TOWN & VILLAGE DISCOVERY TRAILS: Cheshire
Norman James, Abigail Bristow, Tom Hornby & Les Lumsdon

TOWN & VILLAGE DISCOVERY TRAILS: The Yorkshire Dales
Elizabeth Fowler

TOWN & VILLAGE DISCOVERY TRAILS: Staffordshire
Chris Rushton & Les Lumsdon

DISCOVERING COTSWOLD VILLAGES
Gordon Ottewell

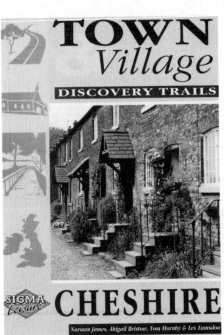

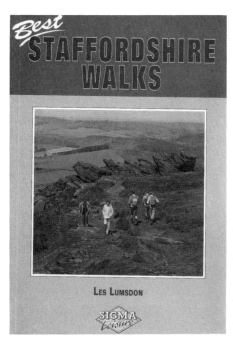

BEST STAFFORDSHIRE WALKS
Les Lumsdon

Popular author Les Lumsdon has completely revised and up-dated his best selling S'taffordshire Walks' to produce this new edition: *£6.95*

BEST PUB WALKS IN THE BLACK COUNTRY
Chris Rushton

The Black Country has plenty of countryside to explore just outside Midlands towns, plus miles of waterway walking *£6.95*

EAST CHESHIRE WALKS:
from Peak to Plain
Graham Beech

Cheshire is so accessible from Staffordshire! This book is now in its THIRD EDITION! Over 200 miles of walks ranging from a three-mile easy saunter to a 20-mile challenge walk over the highest hills! *£6.95*

All of our books are available from your local bookshop. In case of difficulty, or to obtain our complete catalogue, please contact: **Sigma Leisure, 1 South Oak Lane, Wilmslow, Cheshire SK9 6AR Phone: 01625-531035 Fax: 01625-536800 E-mail: sigma.press@zetnet.co.uk** ACCESS and VISA orders welcome. Please add £2 p&p to all orders.